WILL SMITH

FROM FRESH PRINCE TO KING OF COOL

By K. S. Rodriguez

A Division of
HarperCollins*Publishers*

*For John and Mary Lou Squires,
the Fresh Prince and Princess of
Franklin Lakes, New Jersey, and
Ronnie Rodriguez, Man in Blue Suit.*

HarperCollins®, 🖼®, and HarperActive™ are trademarks
of HarperCollins Publishers Inc.

Will Smith: From Fresh Prince to King of Cool
Copyright © 1998 by HarperCollins Publishers Inc.
All rights reserved. No part of this book may be used or
reproduced in any manner whatsoever without written
permission except in the case of brief quotations
embodied in critical articles and reviews. Printed in the
United States of America. For information address
HarperCollins Children's Books, a division of HarperCollins
Publishers, 10 East 53rd Street, New York, NY 10022.

ISBN 0-06-107319-9
Library of Congress catalog card number: 97-77071

1   2   3   4   5   6   7   8   9   10
❖
First Edition

Visit us on the World Wide Web!
http://www.harperchildrens.com

CONTENTS

ACKNOWLEDGMENTS

The author gratefully acknowledges the following people:

Hope Innelli, Lara Comstock, Marco Pavia, and everyone at HarperCollins; Elise Nappi and Lori Levine—thanks for coming through again!; John and Catherine Squires, Arthur Termott, and Christine Squires for their unending support.

1

THE MAN,
THE MUSICIAN,
THE MOVIE STAR

He's one of the most sought-after actors in Hollywood. Two of his movies were the biggest blockbusters of 1996 and 1997, and among the highest-grossing films of all time. His first acting experience was on a top-rated television show. He's also a three-time Grammy-winning rapper. You'd have to be living on Mars not to know who this guy is. And with his reputation among aliens, it's a sure bet that you would have heard about him even then!

This man of many talents is none other than Will Smith, aka the Fresh Prince, Hollywood's leading man of the moment. With an asking price of $20 million per film, Will is now in the same league as Harrison Ford, Sylvester Stallone, and Tom Hanks. But what separates him from the rest of the pack is his sheer versatility.

Will Smith is the only actor to have block-buster films, a top-rated television show, and three Grammy awards under his belt. All this by the astonishingly young age of twenty-eight.

With his bright eyes, winning smile, and infectious sense of humor, Will appeals to all people of all ages and backgrounds. He has grown from a cutup cutie to one of the big screen's sexiest—and highest-paid—leading men.

Will first dazzled us with his talent and charm at the age of nineteen. It was in 1988 that he and his partner, "Jazzy" Jeff Townes, made music history by winning the first Grammy ever presented for rap music. It was also the year they made their first million. With hits such as "Girls Ain't Nothing But Trouble," "Parents Just Don't Understand," and "Summertime," the duo helped usher rap music and hip-hop style onto mainstream radio stations and music-video channels.

With the success of the rap duo DJ Jazzy Jeff and the Fresh Prince, Will's appeal proved so broad that he was given his own sitcom. *The Fresh Prince of Bel-Air* debuted on NBC in 1990 when Smith was just twenty-one years old. The show ran for six seasons and was tremendously popular with audiences old and young, black and white. Smith's great breakthrough helped to pave the way for other rap and R&B stars on television, such as Queen Latifah, Brandy, and LL Cool J.

After conquering the music and television industries, Will hip-hopped to the big screen. He first appeared in small roles in such films as *Where the Day Takes You* and *Made in America*. But it wasn't until his performance in *Six Degrees of Separation* that Will was able to make the film community take notice. In this adaptation of the Tony award–winning play, Smith ventured far from his lighthearted sitcom alter ego to portray a gay con man.

Having caught filmdom's attention, Smith went on to make three blockbusters in a row. *Bad Boys* teamed him with fellow television comedian Martin Lawrence, and took in over $160 million. Will doubled that gross in his next flick, *Independence Day*, which raked in over $300 million in the United States, and $800 million worldwide. But Smith's meteoric rise didn't stop there. His next film, *Men in Black*, topped the U.S. box office charts for 1997, pulling in $249 million. *Independence Day* and *Men in Black* were the biggest movies of 1996 and 1997, respectively, and are among the highest-grossing films of all time.

Men in Black also marked Smith's return to the pop and R&B charts. As the lead singer on the movie's soundtrack, Smith invited listeners to "just bounce it" with him. And they did. The *MiB* soundtrack bounced right onto the airwaves' and the music-video channels' top-ten lists.

Onscreen, this megacool, alien-butt-kicking, overachieving, out-of-this-world superstar has a knack for making everything look easy. But what is the Prince of all media really like offscreen? Even in his personal life, there are many sides to Will Smith. He's a down-to-earth family man, loving father, and devoted new husband to hot young actress Jada Pinkett.

Despite appearances, though, not everything has come easy to Will Smith. Just how did he get his start? What's his magic formula for success? What is he like behind the scenes? What makes his relationship with Jada work? What's next for the rapper/actor/father?

Is it humanly possible for one individual to accomplish all that Will Smith has? Or is Smith really an alien? The answer to all these questions—and more—follow. Read on and find out all there is to know about Will Smith: King of Cool!

2

WILLIE FROM PHILLY

Willard C. Smith II was born September 25, 1968, in West Philadelphia, Pennsylvania, to Carolyn and Willard C. Smith, Sr. He has an older sister, Pam, and two younger siblings, twins Ellen and Harry.

Even as a young boy, Smith loved to laugh and entertain. By all accounts he was a friendly, likable, family-oriented kid. His father, a refrigeration engineer, and his mother, a school administrator, imposed strict but fair values on all the Smith children. Clearly, they taught them how to have lots of fun, too.

Will's parents have described him as a precocious child, a ham who loved performing for his siblings by making faces and getting them into all kinds of trouble for laughing at inappropriate times.

It was hard not to notice the little prince's star quality even then. The family has a video archive of Will as a toddler, hogging the camera. His grandmother must have sensed his blockbuster potential, because she was the one who cast Will in his first roles: the future star appeared in several of her church plays and pageants.

When he was a young boy, Will's interests included dinosaurs, sports, science, math, and especially music. He took piano lessons and claims that other instruments were always strewn about his home. His father would play the guitar, and his mother would sing along.

In addition to encouraging the family's artistic interests, Will's mother pushed her children to do well in school. She valued the importance of a good education and her children were taught always to speak proper English—no street slang was allowed in the Smith household.

Will's mom also taught her children that the classroom wasn't the only place to learn important lessons. For example, one of young Will's greatest learning experiences occurred when he and his family drove cross-country. Stopping at Mount Rushmore, the Alamo, and the Grand Canyon, Will learned firsthand about the scope and splendor of the world. Perhaps it was then that he first became in-spired to conquer it! In any case, the experi-ence was awesome and moving to him. He still likes to visit and share these American wonders with friends to this day.

Will was a smart and clever child who did well in school. He attended Our Lady of Lourdes, a mostly white Catholic junior high, then went to the predominantly black public Overbrook High as a teenager. Although he spent some time in the Catholic school system, Will's family belonged to a Baptist church. In his teens, he hung out with Muslim kids, and lived in a predominantly Jewish neighborhood. He often credits these melting-pot influences with helping him "bridge the gap . . . between the black community and white community" in his music and acting careers.

In high school, Will was best known for his charm and resourcefulness. It seemed as if he could talk his way out of any situation, including missing homework assignments or coming to class late. Will's teachers would call him "Prince Charming" because of his silver tongue. The name caught on and soon everyone started referring to Will by his royal moniker, or by the shorter version, Prince. Will liked the nickname, but added "Fresh" before the Prince "to give it that extra pizzazz," he says.

Will admits that he was the class clown in addition to its smoothest talker. He always enjoyed having fun and making his classmates laugh. "I would talk to someone and get *them* in trouble," he once told Oprah

Winfrey. But he made sure that he had paid enough attention in class to cover himself. If a teacher asked Will a question while he was goofing off, he'd always know the answer and he'd always deliver it in his classic cool style.

Will has described his teen self as energetic, outgoing, and a bit of a nonconformist who enjoyed taking the opposite side of an argument just for fun. He was the type of kid who would dance in the hallways, make noise in the library, or start a food fight in the cafeteria, but still find time to study. With all this fast talking and clowning around, how popular with the girls was he? Surprisingly, Will claims that he didn't date much back then because he was too involved in the rap music world.

Even before he broke into show business, Will dreamed of making it big. His teenage role models and the people he most wanted to be like included Philadelphia natives Guion Bluford, the astronaut, and basketball greats Wilt Chamberlain and Julius "Dr. J" Erving. In fact, outside of his family, Will calls Dr. J the single most important influence on his life while he was growing up.

He also admired stars like Eddie Murphy and Bill Cosby, and proudly followed in their footsteps as a racial-barrier buster in the entertainment field. But Will calls his family the greatest inspiration of all. He is quoted as having said, "There are individual personality traits of celebrities and sports stars and people whom I admire . . . [but] the only people I ever idolized are my parents."

Like many teenagers today, Will was influenced by the culture of the streets. "As an urban kid, I picked up on [rapping]," he has said. "I could put words together well and get a point across with lyrics. It's a natural skill that you have to work on." He'd rap at parties, in school, on the street corners. Soon his persistence paid off. Rap became a way of life for the Fresh Prince of Philadelphia.

As in many cities, the street culture of Philadelphia included crime and drugs. But Will avoided both. He credits his parents with saving him from temptation and peer pressure.

Will's father, a former military man, always made it quite clear that he would not tolerate drug use by his children. Once, he even took Will for a ride through Philadelphia's most squalid neighborhood. "He pointed to the bums sleeping in the doorways and said: 'This is what people look like when they do drugs,'" Will recalls.

"I hated being in trouble," he continues. "I was so petrified of my parents [that] I managed to avoid most pitfalls teens fall in. I just knew when I went to school [that] if a teacher had to call my home, my life was on the line. My father was a serious disciplinarian. I wouldn't dare bring home a D on my report card. The bottom line was no non-sense."

Will once good-naturedly told *TV Guide* that his father wasn't bashful about doling out discipline, and that this discipline was what kept him and his siblings in line. Will describes his dad as "the man with all the answers . . . he did his shaping up by taking little chunks out of your behind."

Discipline and love really worked. Smith says that he's never come close to doing drugs, because of his dad's influence. "There was no peer pressure that was strong enough to [make it worth coming] home and deal[ing] with my father. He wanted to make sure that I knew *he* was my biggest, strongest peer," he told *US* magazine.

Will's father also taught him valuable lessons about hard work and responsibility. One summer, Will Sr. had Will and his younger brother, Harry, tear down and rebuild an enormous, deteriorating brick wall in their yard. It was tedious work that seemed to take an eternity. But when the wall was finished, Will and Harry were proud of their accomplishment. "Dad told me and my brother, 'Now don't you all ever tell me you can't do something.' I look back on that a lot of times in my life when I think I won't be able to do something, and I tell myself, 'One brick at a time.'"

Perhaps that experience also taught the

young men how to work together. Harry is now Will's chief financial officer, and Will's sisters work for him, too. Pam minds Will's interests in Philadelphia, which include an ice-manufacturing company and a charitable foundation, while Ellen works with Harry in Will's L.A. office.

It's a rarity when a family can work so closely—and peacefully—together. But Will's parents had instilled this sense of community in all of their children early on. Will worked alongside his dad repairing refrigeration units when he was in his teens.

It was then that the young upstart learned about the side effects of carelessness. Once, while helping his father with a dangerous wiring job, a tired Will dozed off on the job. He dropped the flashlight he was supposed to be holding so his father could see. Within seconds Will was jarred awake by an ear-piercing scream. "My father sounded like Patti LaBelle," Will jokes now, though he didn't think it was so funny at the time. His father was nearly electrocuted. Will has never forgotten the incident to this day. When he shows up for work now, he always makes sure he is well rested and alert.

Will's father also taught him that focus is another key ingredient to success. "What my father always made clear to me is to just do one thing well. Just concentrate and focus. If you do one thing well, everything else will come from that. I started off rappin' and really concentrated on that. . . . Then the television show came from that and I worked really hard, and the next thing you know I'm doing movies." He adds forcefully, "When you enjoy what you do, you're gonna get good at it."

Sadly, Will's parents separated when he was a teenager. Both, however, were determined to remain heavily involved in his upbringing. Looking back at the breakup, Will has said: "My parents were very loving. We never felt like our parents didn't love us. No matter how difficult things got or how angry someone may have gotten, no matter what happened in our lives, we always felt that we had somewhere to go. You can't spring off into the world from a flimsy base. You've got to have a solid base to jump from."

Will did indeed have a solid base of support. His parents' love contributed greatly to his being an upbeat and good-natured teen. "I was raised in love," he said in *GQ* magazine. "Love of life, love of all people." His parents' unwavering affection also gave him the self-assurance to achieve whatever he put his mind to. "There's a certain level of confidence and self-esteem that comes from knowing for a fact that someone loves you. It's not based on whether or not my homework's done. Just because I'm me, these people love me. So it's like, I know I'm good. How can I let the world know?"

Will's parents must surely be pleased with their self-confident young son now. Loud, energetic, outgoing Willard C. Smith II has put all he has learned to good use and has taken the music, television, *and* movie industries by storm.

3

HE'S THE RAPPER

Will had always gotten good grades, but by the end of high school he was doing especially well in science and math. His parents had visions of him going off to college. In fact, Will was offered a scholarship to attend MIT (Massachusetts Institute of Technology), one of the most competitive and prestigious schools in the country.

But fate had other plans.

Several years earlier, when he was just twelve years old, Will was clowning around at a party, misting "fart spray" at unsuspecting guests. Watching from the other side of the room, Jeff Townes thought it was the funniest thing he had ever seen. He immediately went over to Will to become his partner in crime.

The two boys hit it off and the rest is history.

Jeff was a DJ and Will applied smooth rap rhythms to everything he heard. It was only natural that the two boys would combine their talents. "Everybody has a rap. Rap is the music of the urban black teen," Will explains. "Let's say your friend was to have a party. I have a rap, and there's a DJ, so I'll say my rap. It was just a hobby." The boys called themselves DJ Jazzy Jeff and the Fresh Prince. After playing just a few parties they'd won quite a following.

Will was a natural front man. A born show-off, he had the moves and the look, and people couldn't help but be drawn to him. Jeff remembers Will in those days: "He was the first one to jump off the steps, the first to climb up the trees. Everybody watched and followed later."

What started as simple fun quickly grew into a profitable profession. DJ Jazzy Jeff and the Fresh Prince were soon drawing crowds in local clubs on the Philadelphia rap circuit.

In 1985, when Will was just sixteen, a Philadelphia record producer heard the duo at a club and approached them about cutting a single. Will remembers that the operation was so small, the producer worked out of the trunk of his car! But small or not, the teens jumped at the opportunity to lay down their tracks. They were in business.

Soon the single was being played regularly in the clubs, and then on local rap and R&B

stations. Enter Jive Records: A representative from the label heard the single, and offered to release it nationwide.

Will was excited, but thought they would sell only a few copies. He'd enjoy his fifteen minutes of fame and then go off to college.

He couldn't have been more wrong. The boys' raps were getting play everywhere—not just in their hometown! Their popularity started to skyrocket. Much to his parents' dismay, Will decided that MIT would have to wait.

The following year, in 1986, DJ Jazzy Jeff and the Fresh Prince released the single "Girls Ain't Nothing But Trouble." Shortly after Will's high school graduation, the duo began touring the country. "It was fun," Will recalls. "I thought, if these people are foolish enough to pay me for something I was going to do anyway, then okay."

In 1987 the rappers' first album, *Rock the House,* hit the charts and instantly went gold. The following year, their second album, *He's the DJ, I'm the Rapper*, featured the single "Parents Just Don't Understand" and sold 3 million copies. The single earned the duo a Grammy and a place in rap music history. The growing popularity of rap music, due in part to the success of DJ Jazzy Jeff and the Fresh Prince, led the Grammy committee to create a new award category: Best Rap Performance. Will received the first rap Grammy ever!

One of the highlights of Will's young life was his arrival back in Philadelphia after the ceremony. He and Jazzy Jeff were given a heroes' welcome at the airport. Frenzied fans, family, and even the mayor greeted the duo as they stepped off the plane.

A limousine whisked Will and Jeff to Jeff's mother's house, where she was throwing a celebration dinner party. The two boys were on top of the world. They were an award-winning music sensation, had a hit single, and were still only teenagers! Nothing could burst their bubble.

Nothing, that is, except a reality check from Jeff's mother.

She simply asked them to go out and get her some groceries. Will was taken aback. In his mind, a Grammy-winning rap god didn't have time to go grocery shopping for his pal's mom.

But Jeff's mother insisted. She didn't care *who* they were. As far as she was concerned, they were healthy, able-bodied boys and she needed yams. Will and Jeff were instantly humbled. They slunk out of the house and bought those yams. At that moment, Will realized how his head had grown. He made a promise to never again think that he was too important to do anything for the people he loved. He claims he would still shop for Jeff's mom if she asked.

The Grammy helped DJ Jazzy Jeff and the

Fresh Prince cross over into the pop world, on the airwaves and on the music-video channels, too. Their humorous and playful videos were in heavy rotation everywhere. While most other rappers were posing and chilling in their videos, Will had a very different style. When he wasn't getting punched in the eye, he was being rebuffed by girls!

America warmed to this self-effacing groove. The duo's records continued to climb the charts, beating out lots of other rappers. But Americans weren't the only ones who took notice. When the rest of the world called, the boys answered, embarking on their first international tour.

DJ Jazzy Jeff and the Fresh Prince hit every major hot spot, including London, Moscow, and Japan. Though Will was now world-famous, he never forgot his roots. He still made the time to call and check on his loved ones back in Philly. Sister Ellen says that family-minded Will called home constantly.

What was it that made DJ Jazzy Jeff and the Fresh Prince so popular? Many say it was their sense of humor, but others attribute their success to their clean lyrics. While many artists were rapping about drugs, politics, and violence, Will enjoyed more lighthearted themes.

What the two boys had created was a whole new brand of "fun" rap. Will and Jeff would ultimately catch a lot of flak from other rappers about their style, but Will never paid much attention to that. "It's easy to grab your [crotch] and just spew out misogynist rhetoric. Doing what we were doing—speaking proper English on a rap record, rhyming about being punched in the eye and taking it, not pulling out some giant gun—that's the hard part," he told *Essence* magazine.

Will respects rappers like Ice Cube and the late Eazy-E. He considers them "true poets" who have brought a lot to the genre, but he is also concerned that they may have inspired a slew of rappers he calls "uneducated people with a podium."

He has been quoted as saying, "Somewhere along the line, it became hip to be ignorant. I don't understand that. I don't understand how people can think it's cool not to be articulate. Somewhere along the line, it got cool to be a killer? How can that be cool? That's the most ridiculous nonsense that I've ever experienced in my life." Despite the criticism, Will continued with his own style of rap. And audiences continued to love it.

After the success of 1988's *He's the DJ, I'm the Rapper*, Will and Jeff made an incredibly lucrative career move. During this time, the 900-number phone line business was booming. Will and Jeff were among the first celebrities to record messages for fans to call in and listen to. The response was astounding.

The DJ Jazzy Jeff and the Fresh Prince phone line was the second-highest-grossing line, after the popular Dial-a-Joke. The two made more money from the phone line than they did from their records! Will and Jeff were suddenly millionaires.

Will bought a mansion in Philadelphia, two motorcycles, and six shiny cars. He went on elaborate shopping sprees, buying big gold chains, soft leather jackets, and flashy clothes. Will Smith was rich, famous, and loving it. It seemed like there was nowhere to go but up for the rappers.

Or so he thought. In 1989 the duo released a third album, *And In This Corner*, which featured the popular single "I Think I Can Beat Mike Tyson." And though the record went gold (sold 500,000 copies), Will Smith soon found himself flat broke.

4

RAPS TO RICHES

Sadly, Will Smith lost his first millions as quickly as he made them. He attributes the financial disaster to his immaturity. "I was a moron," he says. "I had the suburban mansion, a motorcycle, I was traveling around the world. I was eighteen and the world was open, and when the world is open like that it makes you crazy, you want everything."

But the winning and the losing led Will to take a hard took at fame and fortune. "I wasn't any happier with money, and I wasn't any less happy when I went broke. It hurt, and mentally it was tough dealing with, but inside it didn't change. I still had my family, and I could still have a good time. I could still laugh."

Will looks back on his wild spending with a bit of humor and a lot of embarrassment. He admits that "money makes people act different." He likes to tell a story about the time he flew from Philadelphia to Atlanta with a bunch of friends just to visit the Gucci store there. The manager closed the place so Will and his posse could shop in peace. But that's not the most extravagant part of the story: There was actually a Gucci shop in Atlantic City, less than an hour away from Philadelphia, that the group could have driven to instead. But the thrill of flying somewhere far away to shop and the excitement of showing off in front of his friends clouded his judgment.

As always, Will's father lent some perspective to the situation. When Will once bragged to his dad about how he had six cars and two motorcycles, his father replied, "What do you need six cars for when you only have one butt?"

Will learned his lesson. He was spending money faster than he was making it and he was drowning in bills. "There's nothing more sobering than having six cars and a mansion one day and you can't even buy gas for the cars the next," he once said. Not only did Will lose many of his possessions, it took him over three years to pay off the debt and back taxes.

"I had to grow up quickly," Will told the *New York Daily News*. "But in a way, I'm glad it happened. In life there are two types of people: those who make mistakes, and keep making the same mistakes over and over again, and those who learn from their mistakes. I like to think I'm the latter."

Will learned other lessons at that time, too. One was particularly brutal. Several of the "friends" who had accompanied him on his wild spending sprees dropped him like a hot potato once his money ran out.

Despite his financial woes, Will didn't despair. He recalled his father's advice about focusing and decided the recording studio was the best place for him to recover from his loss. In 1991 he and Jeff released *Homebase*, which featured the driving single "Summertime." The album and the single went double platinum (sold 2 million copies), and earned them another Grammy for Best Rap Performance by a Duo or Group. Two years later, they followed up with the album *Code Red*, their last collaboration as DJ Jazzy Jeff and the Fresh Prince. *Code Red* didn't sell like their other albums, but by then, restless Will had already sunk his teeth into another medium: television.

5

MR. SMITH GOES TO HOLLYWOOD

Though Will loved life as a rapper, he was ready to branch out into other areas of entertainment. Jazzy Jeff has said that Will wanted to act from the very beginning. In 1990, the Fresh Prince thought the time was right to make that career change, not only because he was eager to reach an even greater audience, but because the extra income would help clean up the financial mess he had made.

It was already apparent from his music videos that Will was a natural in front of the camera. His cockiness and his approachability proved to be the perfect combination. Entertainment industry heads had started noticing this about Will. In fact, he and Jeff had already been offered the lead roles in a rap film, *House Party*.

But Will and Jeff turned down the roles. The movie focused more on rap music than it did on a driving plot. Will didn't want his first movie role to be all about rap. Eventually the movie was cast with another rap duo, Kid n' Play, who modeled the characters in part on Will and Jeff.

Will decided that the best way for him to check out acting and recording prospects was to move to California. So he packed up and headed for Burbank.

The low-key Jazzy Jeff preferred to stay in Philadelphia at the time. The two would still collaborate by fax and phone, and would visit each other often.

Will liked life in California, though he missed his Philadelphia home, family, and friends. He knew Hollywood could be a tough town, but no matter how homesick he became, he wouldn't return to Philly unless he gave acting a true chance.

One day when Will was hanging backstage at *The Arsenio Hall Show*, he struck up a conversation with a young record executive, Benny Medina. As they were making small talk, Benny mentioned that he wanted to get more involved in television. The two talked again later that evening and really hit it off. Will told Medina that he had moved west to break into the acting biz.

Medina was just about to pitch a show to NBC, and he thought Will just might be the perfect guy to star. He told Will that he would be in touch.

The show Benny was going to pitch was based on Medina's own life story. His mother had died when he was young. Consequently he was shuffled from one foster home to another all over Los Angeles. He eventually landed at a juvenile center that was heavily supported by entertainment industry bigwigs. One of them was film and television composer Jack Elliot.

Elliot, who is white, brought Medina, who is black, home to live with his family in Beverly Hills. As fate would have it, Benny Medina went from an unwanted street kid to a student at exclusive Beverly Hills High School—the same school that is portrayed in the popular TV show *Beverly Hills 90210*.

At Beverly Hills High, Benny made friends with lots of kids whose parents had widespread connections in the entertainment industry. Through persistence and hard work, he eventually landed in the record business.

Benny thought his life story would make a terrific sitcom. But he added a twist: What if the family he had moved in with had been black?

Will Smith impressed Medina, who was familiar with the Fresh Prince's music videos and was convinced that Will's hip-hop attitude was right for the show. He later told Bryant Gumbel on the *Today* show that he knew instantly that Will would have "a real appeal on the screen."

Next, Medina set out to interest music and entertainment mogul Quincy Jones in the project. Medina knew Jones from the music business and had heard that Jones was also looking for new television projects. Quincy Jones was the ideal backer for the sitcom, especially with a rap star like Will Smith attached to it.

Medina pitched his idea to Jones, who was already familiar with Smith's music and videos. Quincy agreed that the Fresh Prince was the right man for the job. He told *TV Guide* that he considered Smith "a monster talent."

Next Medina and Jones approached NBC together. The execs were a little reluctant at first. A rap star in a sitcom? That had never been done before. "Can he act?" they asked.

Good question. Medina and Jones had no idea. Smith had absolutely no training, but they were convinced he was a natural because of his music and video background.

NBC gave Medina and Jones the benefit of the doubt, but wanted Smith to come in and audition. By this time, Will was hard to get in touch with. He was playing a few dates across the country with Jeff. Medina ultimately tracked him down in Indiana.

Smith dropped everything and flew back to California for the audition. Even though he had traveled all night and was exhausted, he wowed the NBC bigwigs. Medina remembers the audition like it was yesterday: "He picked up this lousy script and read life into lines he had never seen before, in front of the network brass and everyone. Afterward, I realized I had just sat through one of those moments that people always talk about having. Once he was in front of the camera, he had the ability to completely capture your attention and really hold on to it."

It was clear to the NBC executives that they had just found their next prime-time star. Warren Littlefield, NBC's head of programming at the time, was skeptical until he saw Will's audition. "It was clear to me right away that this guy was a natural. I would go up and down the halls saying we had to do something with him."

NBC jumped on the deal. Will Smith became the centerpiece of the sitcom *The Fresh Prince of Bel-Air*. The show would have a hip-hop sensibility, but it wouldn't be *about* rap. That was exactly the type of role Will was looking for.

On the show, Will played a kid from Philadelphia who moves in with his rich cousins in Bel-Air to escape the gritty streets. His fish-out-of-water character was the first rapper ever to be portrayed on TV. In contrast to Bill Cosby and his preppy sweaters, Will's character wore backward baseball caps, baggy jeans, and high-tops.

"What [fans] can't get on the records is what they'll get on the show," Will told the press. "This is a format I can run wild in and give my fans all the Fresh Prince that they can possibly need."

Brandon Tartikoff, then chairman of the NBC Entertainment group, called Will "the next Eddie Murphy." Needless to say, this generated a lot of hype and raised a lot of expectations. Even Will balked at the comment. "I am nowhere near Eddie Murphy," he said modestly. He wanted to call Eddie directly and tell him it was NBC making the comparisons—though he did add, "Give me four or five years."

It's no wonder that being compared to Eddie Murphy was scary. The older actor was a huge inspiration to Will when he was growing up. "Eddie is the only person that I ever imitated," he recalls. "Eddie inspired a generation of black comedians, in the same way that Richard Pryor [had]. In our lives, we have things that we say that are Eddie Murphy lines from movies. There's probably fifteen or twenty of them that my friends and I say that are just a part of our lives. . . . He's the person that made me see that, okay, maybe I can do this. Because I had never even thought about acting, but seeing Eddie, and being able to be in the mirror delivering Eddie Murphy lines the way he delivers them, made me feel that I could do it."

All the hype petrified the usually self-confident Smith. "I was like, 'Oh please, let me get one episode behind me.'"

Soon every magazine and newspaper in the country wanted to know more about "the new Eddie Murphy." Some were skeptical about the premise of the show—they thought it sounded an awful lot like *The Jeffersons* or *Diff'rent Strokes*. Almost all were doubtful that a rapper could appeal to a prime-time audience on a major network. Most of the press doubted that a rap star could even act.

They would be in for a big surprise.

6

THE FRESH PRINCE OF PRIME TIME

With no prior acting experience, Will Smith crossed his fingers, closed his eyes, and went for it. "Welcome to 50,000 feet," Quincy Jones told him before the series debut.

The Fresh Prince of Bel-Air premiered in the fall of 1990, with costars Tatyana Ali, James Avery, Karyn Parsons, Alfonso Ribeiro, and Janet Hubert-Whitten playing the Banks family, Will's well-to-do television relatives.

The network had taken a risk that quickly began to pay off. *The Fresh Prince of Bel-Air* became number one in its time slot and maintained its high ratings year after year.

NBC had showed a tremendous amount of confidence in Will by giving him a shot at carrying a sitcom. They also allowed him a lot of input for a twenty-one-year-old newcomer. The writers on the show consulted with Will about his character and took his suggestions on dialogue and plot quite frequently.

Despite the sudden stardom in a new medium, Will hadn't forgotten his best friend, Jazzy Jeff. Jeff Townes would appear on the show for most of its six-year run as Will's friend Jazz.

Even though work on the show slowed down Will and Jeff's recording career, it didn't stop the determined duo. They simply recorded during summer hiatuses. It took them a year to complete *Homebase*—with Jeff commuting to Los Angeles from Philadelphia—but they did it. Will cleverly used the show to premiere the video for the Grammy-winning single "Summertime."

But the Fresh Prince's music was not the focus of the sitcom, and Will was quick to point that out. "This is not a rap show by any means. . . . I just happen to have made a couple of records."

Although very few musicians had been able to make the leap from music to television before him, Will wasn't too concerned. "The character is me. I'm not having to do too much acting—I'm just being myself," he admitted to *Interview* magazine in 1990.

When his mother saw the pilot, she laughed. She told Will, "You're not doing anything you never did around here."

Will even found life as a television star less grueling than life as a touring rapper. In the music world, "you work sixteen to eighteen hours a day and never sleep. The lifestyle is a lot harder than TV, where you can at least plan your life."

The other aspect of TV Will enjoyed was the sense of family that both the people and the schedule fostered. Will grew close to many members of the cast and crew—so close that he invited everyone on vacation with him after just one season!

On the set, Will gained a reputation as a jokester. He enjoyed making faces and playing practical jokes on his TV family just as he had on his real-life family. Once he even wrapped all the studio toilet seats in Saran wrap.

At first, he had a great time on the show, but once he noticed the expertise of the other actors, he became a little more self-conscious. It suddenly dawned on him how little he knew about acting. While the other actors had to portray characters, he was essentially playing himself. Everyone else had a wide array of tricks and techniques to use in preparing for their roles.

"I was trying so hard," he remembers. "I would memorize the entire script, then I'd be lipping everybody's lines while they were talking. I can't believe how many mistakes I made. I can't stand to watch myself," he says now in retrospect. "The only thing that saved me on the show was that everybody else in the cast was funny."

Even though Will wasn't quite Laurence

Olivier, movie offers quickly rolled in. In 1991, just one year after *The Fresh Prince* first aired, Will was offered the lead in a science fiction action/adventure film.

Will turned the part down because he felt he wasn't ready yet for the big screen. He hired an acting coach, and the improvement in his skills was soon apparent. As he started to feel more and more comfortable, he experimented with some small film roles. But the payoff for all of his additional training came in 1993, when he was nominated for a Golden Globe as television's best comedy actor.

Will also benefited from the guidance of his esteemed peers in his early television days. Bill Cosby took him under his wing and doled out great advice to the young star. Will recalls one time in particular when he complained to Cosby about writers. The seasoned sitcom star told Smith to go home and try to write his own script.

Will laughed and said that he didn't know how to write a script. Cosby insisted that he try it. He also told him not to sleep until the script was finished.

Will did just that. "When I met the writers the next day, I had a lot less anger and a lot more understanding of the process," he says.

Will claims experiences like that taught him a tremendous amount during his television career. But what was a "learning process" for the young actor turned out to be an incredible smash for NBC.

The show became so popular that entertainment luminaries from various media vied for guest-starring roles. Among the notable guests were Oprah Winfrey, Jay Leno, William Shatner, Quincy Jones, Robin Quivers, Vivica Fox, Tom Jones, B.B. King, Malcolm-Jamal Warner, Jaleel White, Robin Givens, and Vanessa Williams.

Several sitcom hall-of-famers even reprised past television roles to appear on the show. Conrad Bain and Gary Coleman of *Diff'rent Strokes*, and Sherman Hemsley, Isabel Sanford, and Marla Gibbs of *The Jeffersons* all did hilarious cameos.

The Fresh Prince of Bel-Air ran for six seasons, ending in 1996. It was number one with black audiences, and in the top ten overall for a good part of its run.

Will Smith had proved the skeptics wrong. He'd showed the networks that hip-hop culture *could* appeal to the mainstream. Seemingly overnight, Smith had evolved from a simple rap chart-topper to one of America's best-loved prime-time stars.

And he made it look so easy.

7

HIP-HOPPING CAREERS

During the first few years of *The Fresh Prince of Bel-Air*, Will took on a few small movie roles, buying himself some time to learn his craft better. He remembered quite clearly his father's advice about "doing just one thing well" and "focusing." Because he didn't want to fail, he waited for the right starring roles. Instead of grabbing the first thing that came along, Will hung back, and learned about moviemaking "one brick at a time."

His first role was a bit part in the low-budget 1992 film *Where the Day Takes You*, a drama about runaway street kids who form their own "family." The film starred Sean Astin, Lara Flynn Boyle, Ricki Lake, and Dermot Mulroney.

Will played a paraplegic street kid. This relatively small role enabled him to learn about the moviemaking process without taking too much time away from his work on the television show.

There was no turning back from there; Will was bitten by the movie bug.

In 1993 he started filming *Made in America*, a comedy about a woman who tracks down her sperm donor, starring Whoopi Goldberg and Ted Danson. Will played a wisecracking teen who dates Whoopi's daughter. Coincidentally, the daughter was played by Nia Long, who went on to play Will's girlfriend on *The Fresh Prince* from 1994 through 1996.

Made in America wasn't quite the critical success Will had hoped for, but it was a box-office hit. The film raked in $40 million, which meant that a whole lot of Americans were catching Will on the big screen now, too.

But the press began wondering why Will was taking such small parts. After all, his sitcom was a huge success. Surely he had received offers for starring roles!

Will, however, did not give in to their pressure. He preferred to stay on the slow and steady track. "I'm still working on my acting skills," he told the *New York Daily News*. "I feel I've improved, but I'm still not ready to step out with my own feature." This characteristic patience, to hold off on doing something until he could do it perfectly, became a mark of distinction in Will Smith's career.

Will knew that the roles he played in *Where the Day Takes You* and *Made in America* were low-profile, and that suited him just fine. They were real to him and extended a little bit beyond his Fresh Prince persona.

But it was in Will's next movie role, another supporting one, that he would really stretch as an actor.

8
HOTTER THAN 100 DEGREES

I n 1993, Will was cast in the film version of John Guare's Tony award–winning play *Six Degrees of Separation*, alongside film and stage veterans Stockard Channing and Donald Sutherland. He played Paul, a gay con man who talks his way into the homes of Manhattan's upper crust by claiming to be the actor Sidney Poitier's son. The *Los Angeles Times* called his hiring "the most audacious example of Hollywood casting against type since Donna Reed played a hooker in *From Here to Eternity*."

Clearly, this role was a stretch for Will, but it would prove to be the most important one of the young actor's career. "If you lined up a hundred films, this would be the last one people would expect me to do," said Smith. "*Six Degrees* was the scariest choice that I've ever had to make in my career."

Will had good reason to be afraid. None of the roles he had taken till then were quite this demanding or substantial. But something about it just felt right to him. He was convinced he could pull it off. This was his big chance to show the world that he *could* act, that he did have range and versatility.

"In general, television actors don't really get respected in the world of film," he has said. "On *The Fresh Prince of Bel-Air* I never really had an opportunity to show anything beyond telling jokes and having fun and being silly. So there was no reason for anyone to believe that there was any depth beyond that. Just to get *Six Degrees* and to be able to work as hard as I worked was just a really great opportunity for me to prove a couple of people wrong."

Although some speculated that this role might be too tough for him, Will didn't waste a moment listening to naysayers. He thought that if he could just get John Guare to sit down and listen to him, he could at least get an audition.

Guare did agree to visit Will on the set of *The Fresh Prince*, and Will was prepared to make a dazzling pitch to the playwright. But he didn't have to. Guare was won over the minute Will shook his hand and flashed him his now-famous smile.

"I met him with trepidation," the playwright said. "But within five minutes, I was impressed. Except for the charm, the Will I met was not the Fresh Prince. That's one-eighth of what he can do."

Guare immediately suggested Will to director Fred Schepisi. Schepisi couldn't believe that the playwright wanted the Fresh Prince to play Paul. "Everybody got excited about Will," the director remembers, "but I was a little more cautious. I interviewed a lot of actors. But Will tried to convince me that he'd do whatever it would take, would go through whatever process, was sure he could get himself prepared. That confidence and charm was everything the character should be."

It was this confidence that ultimately clinched it for the wary director. Schepisi considered Will's pitch his audition.

Costar Stockard Channing agreed that it was Will's well of confidence that won him the part. "If he had registered any angst or insecurity, he wouldn't have gotten the role."

Will threw himself into his work from the very start, spending three months taking acting and diction lessons before filming began. Like Paul, Smith became a chameleon, someone who could alter his street-kid persona to that of an Ivy Leaguer in a millisecond.

"This character had to learn to walk and talk and act. And I had to learn to walk and talk and act to play him."

For someone who was used to "playing himself" every week on television, this kind of preparation was very intense. "[Playing Paul] was the first time I ever had to be someone else. All of your instincts and all of the things that you've worked on, all the faces you learn to make and all of your go-to tools are stripped. And you're fighting a battle, but you can't use any of the weapons that you've used your whole life, so you have to start from scratch. [*Six Degrees*] is not even comedy and that's what I was used to doing. It was a whole new arena with nothing that I've ever worked with before, not even my own voice. I was taken completely out of my essence. I wasn't able to be me. . . .The role was so different from me that I had to adjust every aspect of myself to play it," he recalls.

None of the training, however, prepared Will for one aspect of the role. As the character Paul, he was asked to kiss a man. Will refused to do it. "You don't see too many rappers playing homosexual roles in films," he explained. "The origins of the music are about masculinity, how tough you can be. So I was concerned about how my credibility would be affected."

Will went to Academy Award winner Denzel Washington for advice about the scene. Denzel thoughtfully told him that it was his commitment to the role that mattered, not the kiss.

Will felt completely committed to the role, yet he still didn't feel right about the kiss.

Schepisi gave in, using fancy camera angles to imply a kiss instead.

In retrospect, Will wishes he hadn't been so squeamish about it all. "I was wrong," he told *US* magazine. "I was definitely wrong." He also explained in *Ebony* magazine that "I learned a valuable lesson in that you do the audience a disservice if you don't completely commit to the character. If you are not going to commit, then don't take it."

Will says that he feels his performance would have been much stronger had he done the kiss. "It was very immature on my part. . . . I was thinking, 'What are my friends in Philly going to think about this?' I wasn't emotionally stable enough to artistically commit to that aspect of the film."

But audiences didn't seem to notice anything was missing. They were astonished by Will's top-notch performance. His work in this film earned him the respect of Hollywood, too. He showed the film community he could shed his Fresh Prince image to take on just about any role.

Will credits his coaching and his costars with helping him fill the role so completely. Neither Donald Sutherland nor Stockard Channing had ever heard of Will Smith before they worked with him, but that didn't prevent them from lending the young actor support.

Channing had already won a Tony for her

performance in the Broadway play. "Stockard was really great because she was like an encyclopedia of *Six Degrees*," Will told the *Today* show. "She had done it with so many different people, so many different times, that if I was feeling a little uncomfortable about something, she knew five or six ways that other people had tried it. All of the problems that I may have had, she had already discussed with people previously doing the role. So she was very clear about what she wanted to do, and she was very open about things that she had experienced with it."

For example, in the film there is a telephone scene that runs thirty pages in the script. Smith obsessed about memorizing every word, like he was used to doing on *The Fresh Prince*. But Channing told him, "Let's make this scene play off of each of us rather than the words. Don't worry about the words, just understand the emotion."

Improvisation? Ad-libbing? These were skills Will had never used before on *The Fresh Prince of Bel-Air*. He had clearly come a long way from his sitcom character. After the film opened, Channing praised the young actor, as did Sutherland, who called Will "wonderful."

Kudos started to come in from all over. Playwright John Guare was immensely happy with Will's performance, saying that he truly captured "the range of [Paul]: from the home-boy to the Harvard senior."

Fresh Prince costar James Avery says that *Six Degrees* was Will's best performance ever. "I think there's a lot more going on there than anyone knows. I think there is a lot more going on there than *he* really is aware of."

Director Barry Sonnenfeld, who would later work with Smith on *Men in Black*, said he couldn't believe Will wasn't nominated for an Oscar. In any event, Will felt he'd walked away from the project with something far more valuable than an Oscar—he had finally attained the knowledge and experience he had been seeking all along.

But the experience was not without its difficulties. Returning to the set of *The Fresh Prince* after such a growth spurt proved to be tough for Will. "I grew tremendously as an actor [doing *Six Degrees*], but at that time I didn't realize how far you could get lost in a character, and I got so far into the Paul character that when I came back for the fourth season, I was lost, I didn't know what I was doing. I didn't know who my character was, I didn't know how to talk or how to stand or any of that stuff. I lost the character [of the Fresh Prince]."

Will had just begun to understand how enormously different the two mediums, film and television, could be. But he firmly believed TV gave him his edge. On the set of a television show, "You've got five days, period. You get in the habit of doing things, creating things, quickly. . . . When you get into a movie . . . the tempo is much slower, but your mind is still going a million miles a minute, so you end up pitching more, and getting more things done. It's so much easier to find that great line, or that great delivery, in that form. You get more time, and there's a lot more space to achieve that perfection."

Will also says the sitcom experience taught him to "maximize every single moment. That's why TV actors pop on film screens, especially TV comics."

Will noticed another difference between television and the big screen: "You get the immediate feedback of a live audience in television, which is really great—you know instantly whether it's right or wrong. The difference with making films is you have more of an opportunity to get it right."

Will did admit that the slow-moving pace on a movie set sometimes made it difficult to keep his energy up. But he liked the opportunity to become "someone else" that movie-making offered him.

By 1993, Will Smith had caught the attention of many big-league movie producers and directors, though he had only appeared in three films. His hard work in *Six Degrees* had made a big impression and proved that he was big-screen material.

He was ready to move into the realm of big-budget, high-profile blockbusters. He would not only have the starring role, he would prove to be a bona fide box-office draw.

But before he would accomplish that, there were other things Will had to attend to in life: marriage and fatherhood were two of those things. These experiences would teach Will more about living than making movies ever could.

9

FROM PRINCEHOOD TO PARENTHOOD

Everything in Will Smith's life seemed to be moving full steam ahead during the early nineties, including his love life. Touring on the road as a rapper had made it difficult for him to have serious relationships, but life as a television star allowed him to stay in one place long enough to make that goal a reality.

When Will first moved to California, he dated and moved in with a model. She soon dumped him for a major R&B artist, but Will wasn't down for long. He used his characteristic humor to get through the disappointment. He even joked about it on *The Arsenio Hall Show.*

After that, Will kept a low romantic profile. Then in 1991, while visiting a friend on the set of the sitcom *A Different World,* he met Sheree Zampino, a fashion design student. As they talked and got to know each other better, Will found that he had fallen head over heels for the dark-eyed beauty. But while it was love at first sight for Will, it took a little more time for Sheree to feel the magic. Will had to do some sweet talking before she would even go out with him.

After many phone calls from her new suitor, Sheree decided to give in to Will's persistence. Before long, she was under his spell. The couple's relationship grew serious quickly, and less than a year after they met, Will proposed marriage.

"It was Christmas Eve [1991]," Will told *TV Guide*. "[Sheree] was in Los Angeles and she thought I was flying to Philadelphia to spend Christmas with my family. What I actually did was go to the airport to meet my brother. He had flown in to bring me the ring I'd bought from a friend of mine in Philadelphia. Then I went home and called [Sheree] and told her that I'd forgotten some important papers. Could she please go to my house and grab them for me? I really needed these papers. So she drove there, and when she got inside I was waiting for her in the bedroom on one knee with the ring, and I proposed to her there."

The two were wed in May 1992. Both were twenty-three years old. The reception was held at the Four Seasons Biltmore Hotel in Santa Barbara, California, after the couple said their vows overlooking the Pacific Ocean at the luxurious hotel. Denzel Washington and "Jazzy" Jeff Townes were among the 125 people who attended.

Since Sheree was studying fashion design, she chose the perfect gown to match Will's elegant tuxedo. It was designed by Renee Strauss, who designed the wedding dress for the remake of the film classic *Father of the Bride*.

Ebony magazine named the newlyweds one of the "ten hottest couples." They spent a few blissful months attending premieres hand in hand, vacationing together, and enjoying quiet time in their new home.

Then in December they became the proud parents of Willard C. Smith III, whom they nicknamed Trey. Will and Sheree were ecstatic at the birth of their beautiful new son.

Will recalls how fatherhood changed his outlook on life. "When the doctor handed him to me, I realized things were different now. Suddenly I felt a *huge* yoke of responsibility. I have to wear my seat belt now and things like that—work out, stay healthy, eat right—because it's not just for me anymore."

Will continues, "I've always had a fast-car, no-seat-belt attitude. Now I'm slowing down a bit." And he wasn't kidding. During the car ride home from the hospital, Will was a nervous wreck, realizing that a tiny, fragile person was his passenger. This new responsibility led him to move out of the fast lane, not only in his car but in life in general.

Will says fatherhood has made him more careful and thoughtful. "The decisions that I made and will make will just affect his life forever," he once told Oprah Winfrey on her show.

Although Will enjoys parenting, his eyes are fully open to its challenges. He says that when he was growing up, he always believed his parents were completely in control and knew everything. Now he realizes that wasn't always true. His parents had to wing it a lot. These are skills he's learning now, too.

It was soon after Trey's birth that Will took on the role in *Six Degrees of Separation*. Though it was an important career move, Will now says it wasn't the best thing for his marriage.

He became so intensely involved in getting his part right that his relationship suffered. The neglect Sheree felt was understandably hard to endure, and especially hard to empathize with since she didn't have a career in the entertainment field.

"I didn't know that when you work on a role that hard, it gets inside of you, that it makes you crazy, puts you in a different place," Will explained. "When I was doing the character, I *became* him for a little while. I would block out seventy-two hours and try and shop like he would shop—just *be* him. Sheree and I were newlyweds, and I was basically crazy."

Smith also added that so many things were occurring in their lives at once, both he and Sheree had trouble dealing with it all. "We had a new son, and my career was taking off. There was lots of pressure that didn't allow the marriage to blossom."

The couple stayed together though they weren't happy. They gave it their best shot, and Will was determined to keep their love alive for the sake of Trey. But it still didn't work. Sheree filed for divorce in 1995 after three years of marriage.

The split shattered Will. For the first time, he felt he had failed at something, and it was something as important as a marriage. Will says regretfully, "I really believe that a man and woman together, raising a family, is the purest form of happiness we can experience." He claims he would have stayed in the unhappy marriage years longer for the sake of his son, Trey.

But Will couldn't blame Sheree for wanting out. "It's not the perfect situation," he says of the breakup, "but that's what life has dealt. We all make mistakes, and we have to find the good thing out of it. What was a mistake for me created the most beautiful thing I've ever seen in my life," he says, referring to his son.

Looking back, Will admits that perhaps he and Sheree married too young and too quickly.

No matter what the cause, the divorce also affected Will tremendously on a professional level. He believes the distraction it caused him contributed to a particularly weak season of *The Fresh Prince of Bel-Air* and that it hindered his musical creativity as well, explaining his four-year absence from recording from 1993 to 1997.

Will made sure that Trey would be well provided for in his divorce settlement. In addition to child support, Will contributes annually to a trust fund for Trey's education.

Although he and Sheree agreed to share custody of Trey, it still pains Will that Trey won't grow up with both parents in one household. "To me, a child being able to hear the thunder outside and to run and jump into bed with his mother and father . . . that's a memory my son will never have . . . my son will never experience some of the beauty that I experienced of having a family."

But Will, Trey, and Sheree cope. As Will says, "Trey has a mommy and a daddy and there are two separate houses and that's just what his life is. It isn't the optimum situation, but that's his reality."

Though Will's parents divorced when he was a teenager, they were together during his formative years. Even after the divorce, his father lived close by and was always around. Because of this, Will knows the importance of a father figure in a child's life. He plans on being around for Trey—always.

Will's a doting dad who spends the bulk of his free time with his young son. He'll frequently bring Trey to the set of the movie he's currently working on.

Costar Alfonso Ribeiro recalled that when Trey visited the set of *The Fresh Prince of Bel-Air,* he was extremely well behaved and polite. "He'd ask, 'Excuse me, can I play with this?' He knew about the bell that went off when we started taping. When he heard it, Trey would put his finger to his mouth and say, 'Shh!'"

Fatherhood has brought out tender emotions in Will that he had never before experienced. Trey once smashed a mug through a window: Will smacked him on the hand, and Trey started to cry. Will, relieved that the shattered glass hadn't harmed his son, then sent Trey to his room. When he was alone, Will himself broke down and cried. Disciplining his son hurt more than he could have imagined. Will thought how tough it must have been for his own father trying to handle four children.

Another time, Will was overcome when Trey was saying his prayers before going to sleep. He came to the part about "If I should die before I wake," and Will started crying at the mere thought of losing his son. Will slept cradling Trey for the rest of that night.

Though Will finds parenting hard, he is a beaming father. Now he has baby number two on the way with his new wife, Jada Pinkett.

Will's philosophy on parenting is similar to his own parents' philosophy: "There's three things that you can give your child," he says. "You give them love, you give them knowledge, you give them discipline. You give your kids those three things, and everything else is in the hands of the Lord."

10

KEEPING THE FRESH PRINCE FROM GETTING STALE

L ike all good things, *The Fresh Prince of Bel-Air* finally came to an end. "We had a nice run," Smith says.

Bigger and better movie roles were being offered to Will, and soon television seemed too confining. He sought a medium where he could stretch his performance skills. "[In a TV series] you're pretty much the same old, same old. And I wanted to go out while we were good. You get up to eight or nine seasons and then you're struggling. I wanted to go out solid, while we were still funny."

Even the Fresh Prince persona was wearing thin for him. "When I started doing *The Fresh Prince of Bel-Air*, I was twenty years old. Inside those [six] years, I went through three careers, music, television, movies. I got married, had a baby, divorced. It's like I did a whole lot of living in that time. My life experiences are so far advanced beyond the character's life experiences. It was almost like a regression for me to play the character."

Ending the show was certainly bittersweet for Will. He had grown so attached to the cast and crew. "We had a ball. The people start to take on the surrogate roles of the characters, you start to have those kind of concerns for the people that you work with. It's like leaving a family, more than just leaving a job."

When Sherman Hemsley, best known for the hit sitcoms *The Jeffersons* and *Amen*, guest-starred on *The Fresh Prince of Bel-Air*, he told Will that it was best to end the show while it still had some steam. Hemsley recalled how he'd found out about the demise of *The Jeffersons*. He showed up for work one day and his parking spot was gone.

Will took Hemsley's advice and decided that he wanted to "go out standing." He didn't want the show to become known as "*The Stale Prince of Bel-Air*," and it was time for him to move on.

After Will and company taped the final episode, the gang had a party where they celebrated with a huge cake—and a food fight of similar proportions.

Though Will tried his best to keep the tears at bay, creator Benny Medina says he wasn't successful. "He was dazed in a way. He had this kind of look I've seen when something deep is going on, but he doesn't want to let on what's going on for fear it'll cause someone else to become emotional. I was probably the first person to see him after he did his last scene for the series. He walks through the empty house, then leaves, and I saw him come off the set and his eyes were full of tears."

Fresh Prince fans can still catch the show in syndication—in some areas it airs as many as three times a day. While it went into reruns, Will Smith's career seemed to fast-forward. He went on to accomplish something only a few select television stars have been able to.

In the elite tradition of Robin Williams, John Travolta, Jim Carrey, and Bruce Willis, Will Smith soared from prime-time prince to bona fide box-office big shot.

11

THE LEAP TO LEADING MAN

After his success in *Six Degrees of Separation*, Will decided to focus more on the big screen. With *The Fresh Prince of Bel-Air* on its way out, now was the time for him to make the leap to leading man.

Offers flooded in, so Will could be choosy. He had wanted to play a role that fell somewhere between the ones he played on *The Fresh Prince* and in *Six Degrees*. One script especially appealed to him. It was for a film titled *Bad Boys*.

Bad Boys was a buddy-cop film originally intended to be a vehicle for *Saturday Night Live* alums Dana Carvey and Jon Lovitz. But the producers—Don Simpson and Jerry Bruckheimer—decided to add a twist to this action/comedy. Thinking back to Simpson and Bruckheimer's earlier hit *Beverly Hills Cop*, which starred Eddie Murphy, the producers wanted their hero cops to be black.

Will was a little concerned about the movie looking too much like a *Beverly Hills Cop* rip-off, but when he read the script closely, he saw that the emphasis was really more on the action than the comedy. The treatment was different enough from comedian Eddie Murphy's hit to warrant further consideration.

Will also liked the prospect of playing a cop. This would be his first starring role in a film, and he felt comfortable in the comedic territory, though it wasn't the situational comedy of *The Fresh Prince of Bel-Air*. This time, Will's character was an action hero. He could flex his muscles and set up jokes at the same time!

When Will learned that fellow sitcom star Martin Lawrence was going to play his partner, he decided to take the role.

Bad Boys is about a mismatched cop team in Miami who must recover $100 million worth of heroin in seventy-two hours. Will plays detective Mike Lowrey, the playboy to Martin Lawrence's family man, detective Marcus Burnett. While Will was used to mugging for the camera on *The Fresh Prince*, that task fell to Lawrence in *Bad Boys*. Will was thrilled to finally play the straight man.

And playing a hero in *Bad Boys* was a lot of fun for Smith. He had never been able to run, jump, and "dive-roll into a split and tackle the bad guys" before.

Just how well did the two stars get along? Wonderfully. They had met only once before, at an awards show. When they became re-acquainted on the movie set, they clicked instantly.

In *Vibe Online* Martin said of his collaboration with Will: "You never see two brothers from different networks getting together to do something like this. We had a lot of fun. We worked hard together. Since both of us have comic timing on the sitcoms, we knew it was just a matter of getting together and finding out how we complemented each other."

Will says that Martin "had a lot of interesting insights. I called him Martin Lawrence King. It's really important to him to be real, and present himself and his work to his audience with integrity."

Because Lawrence and Smith were established comedians, the scriptwriters left a lot of the humor open to be improvised by them. That could have led to a sticky situation if the costars had giant egos and tried to one-up each other. But that wasn't the case with these two hotshots at all.

"From day one," Smith told Bryant Gumbel on the *Today* show, "we completely left everything open for the other guy. . . . We never had a problem with that. It wasn't fighting for screen time. It was more offering your screen time and letting it fall on the character that it better suited."

Will compared this kind of improvisation to "a tennis match. [Martin] would say something, then I'd toss a line right back." He often said that Martin's comic timing was expert. "Martin is a comedic genius. In fact, he's a comedic geyser."

With a budget of $23 million, a lot was riding on the success of the film. But the movie exceeded all of Columbia Pictures' expectations, earning a whopping $140 million. It turned out to be one of the biggest box-office hits of 1995. Not too bad for two first-time feature cops.

Will enjoyed working with Martin Lawrence so much that he made a cameo appearance in Martin's next film, *A Thin Line Between Love and Hate*. Will has also been quoted as having said that he'd be happy to do "*Bad Boys 16* and *17* thirty years from now."

And he wasn't joking, either. The pair signed on the dotted line for *Bad Boys 2* before there was even a script. Neither star seems very concerned about the absence of a plotline. As Smith has said, "With these action movies, the thing you have to get right is your bad guy—your movie is only as good as your bad guy. You get your bad guy right and you get your explosions right. Martin and I will take care of the rest."

It appears that Will Smith was well cast in *Bad Boys*. *Entertainment Weekly* noted that "Smith . . . holds the camera with his matinee-idol sexiness and his quicksilver delivery of lines." But *People* magazine summed it up best: "Smith is an actor with a refined sense of comedy." It was the movie that put him on the map as one of the most dynamic action heroes Hollywood has ever seen. Little did Hollywood know that the talent Will showcased in *Bad Boys* was only the tip of the iceberg.

12

WILL SMITH SAVES THE WORLD

By 1995, it seemed as if Will Smith had accomplished everything. *Six Degrees of Separation* proved that he could act, and *Bad Boys* showed that he could draw a $100 million crowd. But what happened next exceeded everyone's expectations.

Right after *Bad Boys*, Will was cast in a movie that would propel him into a whole different sphere of success. *Independence Day* shot him straight into superstardom and made him one of Hollywood's most sought-after leading men.

In *Independence Day*, Will plays Captain Steven Hiller, a cocky fighter pilot who saves the world from alien attack. The film features a first-rate ensemble cast, including Jeff Goldblum, Judd Hirsch, Randy Quaid, Mary McDonnell, Bill Pullman, and beautiful Vivica Fox as Will's girlfriend. Will compared working with the cast of *ID4*, as it became known, to playing basketball with Michael Jordan. He told Oprah Winfrey that working with excellence inspired him to be the best he could be.

Will was thrilled to participate in *Independence Day*. He had so much fun doing *Bad Boys* that he was eager to make another action film. Plus, he's an admitted science fiction fan, claiming that he grew up watching *Star Trek* and reading comics like *X-Men* and *Ultraman*.

ID4 promised to be one of Hollywood's biggest films ever. Working on a film of that size would be a first for Will, and he loved every minute of it. "I like the genre of the 'big-budget-Hollywood-blow-'em-up-shoot-'em-up' movie," he says. "That's fun for me. It's physical. You get to do stunts and all that. Making movies is kind of like choosing a sport. . . . It's an enjoyable thing. My job is fun. So it all depends on what kind of fun I feel like having today."

Independence Day captivated audiences with its scary premise and amazing special effects. Imagine aliens hovering over—and then destroying—New York City. It's the uncertainty of what lies in the cosmos that attracts—and frightens—audiences. Will calls *Independence Day* "a disaster film in the classic sense . . . you don't know who is going to be around at the end." He even prepared for filming by watching the epic disaster flick *The Poseidon Adventure* over and over.

ID4 was made in fourteen months, with a budget of $71 million—surprisingly cheap for a Hollywood film of these proportions. When the year's box-office receipts were tallied, it was 1996's biggest moneymaker, raking in over $300 million domestically, and $800 million worldwide.

The film featured over five hundred special effects shots that used more than six thousand elements. Many of Will's scenes were acted with aliens, which wasn't as easy as one might think. "If you're acting with an alien," he told *Boxoffice Online*, "it's a mark on the floor or something. And it's [filmed] in such small pieces you can never really get a good run at a scene. So it's difficult finding the moments. . . . On the set they'll say, 'Okay, look to the left and just say your line to the left,' and you're like, 'What the heck is that for?' But when you see it all together, it's amazing."

While the film's creatures and special effects, such as an exploding White House, provided to be incredibly popular with the public, the movie's director, Roland Emmerich, also credits Will with much of the film's appeal. "Audiences identify with him," he said. "I'd see it in their eyes at test screenings."

Emmerich says he brought Smith into the film because he was tired of the blond, blue-eyed cliché of the All-American soldier. "He's much more interesting a performer [than that]," the director said, then prophetically added, "He's going to be huge."

That was an understatement. Will brought a real down-to-earth sensibility to the macho role. He also brought his sense of humor to the set. At one point, he and costar Jeff Goldblum started laughing uncontrollably. "It was just one of those bizarre nights. It was about midnight," Smith recalled in the *Los Angeles Times*, "we had been there all day, and now we're expected to save the world. It was really bizarre because *everything* was hilarious. The seriousness of saving the world became hilarious. It got to be so funny. We're looking at each other and cracking up, like, 'Who the hell would pick you to save the world? You were the Fly, for God's sake!'" Smith said, referring to Goldblum's role in the remake of the classic sci-fi flick.

Even with the occasional laughing fit, Smith was always professional. He really took the role seriously, putting a lot of time, energy, and dedication into making his character convincing. To prepare for the role of Captain Hiller, Smith even trained with a Marine lieutenant, who filled him in on the basics of flying.

He also used one of his all-time favorite sci-fi heroes, Harrison Ford's Han Solo in *Star Wars*, as a point of reference. Will thought that Hiller and Solo had a lot in common, and

Will Smith's character in *Men in Black* may have zapped people's memories, but he still has the most unforgettable smile on the planet. (© 1996, Ron Davis/Shooting Star)

On his way to the top of the music world, Grammy-winning rap artist Will Smith kicked out the jams with his musical partner, DJ Jazzy Jeff. You knew him then as Fresh Prince.
(© 1993, Ron Wolfson/London Features)

Seven years ago he posed for the "I could definitely get used to this lifestyle" picture above. Now asking for $20 million per movie, he definitely did get used to this lifestyle! (© 1990, NBC/Globe Photos)

Will Smith is pictured here with his old television family, the cast of "The Fresh Prince of Bel-Air." (© 1993, NBC/Shooting Star)

Influential producer Quincy Jones was one of the people who helped give Will his start in acting. (© 1990, Sylvia Sutton/Globe Photos)

In *Independence Day*, Will saves the world from an alien invasion—just in time for a 4th of July barbecue. Go Will! (© 1996, Twentieth Century Fox/Shooting Star)

Man in black, boy in black. Trey takes his real-life role as Will Smith's son very seriously. (© 1997, Lisa Rose/Globe Photos)

Will poses with two leading ladies, his Mom and actress Jada Pinkett.
(© 1995, Ron Davis/Shooting Star)

When Hollywood wants to make a blockbuster movie they always call in the big guns. Will is pictured here with his *Men in Black* co-star Tommy Lee Jones. (© 1997, Columbia-Tristar/Shooting Star)

With so much experience in front of the camera at such a young age, will Will flip sides to stand behind the camera, too? Could directing really be in his future?
(© 1997, Theo Kingma/Shooting Star)

Will was all smiles after winning this honor at the 3rd Annual Blockbuster Awards in Hollywood. He added this award to his collection, which includes three Grammys, an MTV Best Kiss Award, and four NAACP Image Awards. Can an Oscar be far off?
(© 1997, Steve Granitz/Retna Ltd.)

Although Will's fans come in all ages, he loves pleasing kids most. They showed their appreciation by honoring him at the 1997 Nickelodeon Kids' Choice Awards.
(© 1997, Terry Lilly/Shooting Star)

The couple in white smiles down the aisle at their New Year's Eve 1997 wedding.
(© 1997, AP/Wide World Photos)

he studied the nuances of heroism versus humor that Ford brought to the character. "The role is interesting because it's definitely serious, but he's also able to be funny. I'd never experimented with that before; it's either been one or the other."

Bringing both elements to Captain Hiller made playing the part easier and much more enjoyable than he expected it to be. "Everybody has an action hero in them; everyone wants to kick in a door and shoot somebody."

What makes Smith's action heroes stand out is his ability to craft a character audiences can relate to. He firmly believes that audiences identify better with reluctant heroes. He knew he had to make Hiller "as real as possible, because what makes you an effective superhero is that you don't want to be one. Like Bruce Willis in *Die Hard*—the last thing he wanted to do was run over that glass barefoot. People can't relate to a guy who just jumps in front of bullets."

Will made Hiller real by making him funny, reluctant, and brave all at the same time. Will's Hiller is part Eddie Murphy, with wisecracks about kickin' E.T.'s butt, part wary Bruce Willis, who would rather not be doing this at all, and part Wesley Snipes, the guy with a beefed-up bod pumped full of bravery.

This unique combination not only made Smith a hero to thousands of moviegoers, it made him a sex symbol, too. Soon women were mobbing him wherever he went. Smith recalls one woman who spotted him while she was driving. She kept her eyes on Will instead of the road and crashed into another car. When she jumped out of the car, she didn't stop to look at the damage. Instead, she ran after Will to get his autograph!

Another time, a woman came up to him in a record store and asked him to sign his autograph—on her body! He claims he's even had toothless old women plant unsolicited kisses right on his lips! Will's appeal knows no limitations.

Why does Will Smith think he's become so popular? He offers an easy answer: "I think I'm probably the first black guy that ever saved the world."

13

WILL SMITH SAVES THE WORLD— AGAIN!

After *Independence Day*, Hollywood producers and directors were banging down Smith's door. One of the most relentless was Steven Spielberg.

Spielberg was developing a movie called *Men in Black*, with director Barry Sonnenfeld, of *Addams Family* and *Get Shorty* fame. The film was to be more lighthearted and humorous than the dark comic book on which it was based.

Men in Black, the film, is about federal immigration agents who crack down on illegal aliens—from space—who are using the planet Earth as a way station. Some aliens assimilate into the human population nicely, performing services valuable to Earth's original inhabitants. The film suggests that there are aliens among us everywhere. How else does one explain the existence of Dennis Rodman, Newt

Gingrich, or weatherman Al Roker? Other aliens, however, pose a deadly threat to the human population. These are the outlaws that the Men in Black have been recruited to hunt down.

Sonnenfeld says he was instantly attracted to the project. "I loved its sensibility because I've always believed deeply in my heart that we as humans really don't have a clue about what's going on. I loved the fact that I could make a movie, play it for the reality of the situation, with aliens in it, and let the world know that perhaps we truly don't have a clue."

Spielberg had already convinced Oscar-winner Tommy Lee Jones to take on the role of stone-faced Agent K. But he still needed an actor to play his sidekick, Agent J. People involved in the project pitched Spielberg names like Chris O'Donnell and Brad Pitt.

But Spielberg was looking for an actor with a unique set of skills. Agent J had to have good comic timing *and* broad appeal.

After a screening of *Independence Day*, Spielberg knew he had found his man in Will Smith. "He's a totally honest actor," Spielberg said. "He's funny and he's serious all rolled into one. . . . I thought he would make a great J."

When Spielberg called, Smith didn't jump at the role right away. Although he greatly respected Steven Spielberg, Will was reluctant to do another alien movie right after *Independence Day*. After all, he had carefully chosen his other roles so that he wouldn't be typecast and forced to play the same part over and over again.

But Spielberg wouldn't let up. He wanted to talk to Smith about the project in person. Whisked to Spielberg's Long Island home by helicopter, Will was presented with a $12 million offer.

Spielberg sat Smith down and explained how *Men in Black* would be different from *Independence Day*. Smith listened carefully, still not entirely convinced that making two alien flicks in a row was a good move for him.

But then Smith realized that one simply couldn't say no to the genius behind such blockbusters as *Jurassic Park* and *E.T.* Smith explains that it wasn't the money or the concept that won him over. When Spielberg told Smith who else was involved in the project, he didn't need any more convincing. "Ninety percent of making a movie is the team. It's Barry Sonnenfeld, Tommy Lee Jones, and Steven Spielberg. You can't beat that team. So I was in."

Spielberg knew the decision to cast Smith was a good one. The famous director often uses his kids as a barometer of star quality. And Will Smith rated the highest with them.

Spielberg told Oprah Winfrey that his kids "don't show up for anybody [even though we've] had a few movie stars cross our welcome mat. [But] they were part of the entire meeting. They sat right there on the couch staring at this man."

Smith clicked right into the character of Agent J, who is a New York City cop enlisted by Agent K (Tommy Lee Jones) to become a Man in Black. "J is the kind of character who enjoys life and experiencing new things," Will said. "He also thinks he's the smartest person in the world, so becoming an MiB is the ultimate challenge. Adapting to this new world really drives this character, and the same thing that made him want to be a police officer, to be the guy who serves and protects, is now what makes him want to join the ultimate police force."

Serving and protecting may sound a lot like Captain Steven Hiller, the role Smith played in *ID4*. But Smith insists that the characters are different. "The whole posture, the walk, and all of that stuff is completely different. With [J], how he sits in a chair, and the whole attitude, is that New York cop kind of thing."

Even though Agent J looks at Agent K as "kind of a grump," Smith loved working with Tommy Lee Jones. "He's completely dead-pan and straight," Smith says. "We had a ball working together."

Smith learned a lot from watching Jones. He told *CBS This Morning* that Jones was a "brilliant technical actor . . . he knows everything that's going on on the set—the lights and the cameras; he knows how everything works, in order to put himself in a position to have his greatness captured."

He has also praised Jones for his exceptional comic timing. "He would toss me soft pitches that I could smack out of the ballpark," Smith said. "Just lobbin' those jokes up there for me."

Director Sonnenfeld gave the pair a lot of leeway with the dialogue of the film, which Smith felt worked out well. "Barry was really loose with Tommy and me and allowed us to make the characters our own. We just had fun, man," Smith says of the collaborative effort.

Like *Independence Day*, *Men in Black* featured some amazing special effects. Once again, Will found himself acting alongside creatures from another planet who weren't there. "I'm an expert now," he joked in *Mr. Showbiz Online*, "but special effects work is so tedious. It's difficult to get a performance right because it's so technical. You have to get your head a certain way, then your arm has to be up a certain way when you're talking to the alien . . . and it's one line at a time. You gotta pay so much attention to saying it at the right tempo, and at the right time, that you can't really concentrate on being normal."

For example, Smith describes a shot that has "fifty aliens . . . and everything has to line up properly, and there's guys walking on the ceiling, and guys levitating, all this stuff in one shot—and dialogue. So it's like shooting and shooting and shooting and shooting. It may take us two days to get fifteen seconds of what's going to be in the movie."

Despite the difficulties, Smith turned in a performance that was out of this world.

14

THE TWENTY-MILLION-DOLLAR MAN

Independence Day had opened on the Fourth of July weekend in 1996; *Men in Black* opened exactly one year later. "I own that weekend—that's mine," Smith likes to joke. And just like *ID4*, *MiB* was a tremendous success. The film—and Will—won rave reviews.

USA Today called it an "*Independence Day* for smart people." Their critic even went so far as to say, "Smith is so appealingly cool it should be illegal."

Joel Siegel of *Good Morning America* said of *Men in Black*: "This is the one that's worth waiting in line to see, the one you'll want to see two or three times. . . . Will Smith makes everything look great. He is the real thing, a star, smart. You can't tell he's acting. There's something about him you just want to like. And as a bonus, he's dynamite with a punch line."

Critical acclaim wasn't the only thing pouring in that first weekend. *Men in Black* set the record as the highest-grossing film to open on the July 4 weekend ever, earning $51.1 million and surpassing its predecessor, *Independence Day*.

After only five days in release, the film had brought in $84.1 million, the largest five-day dollar amount next to *The Lost World: Jurassic Park*. *MiB* went on to surpass the monstrous success of the dinosaur sequel, earning over $220 million in just eight weeks. It became the highest-earning movie of 1997, at $313 million worldwide.

MiB fever quickly swept the nation. People couldn't see the movie enough times. Kids flocked to toy stores to buy *MiB* action figures—yes, there is a Will Smith doll out there! And an *MiB* animated series was launched in the 1997–98 TV season.

There is talk of a sequel, but don't expect it to be too soon. Will explains that he doesn't want audiences looking at him as "That Alien Guy" and jokes that he doesn't "want the aliens to think that either."

Men in Black also rekindled part of Will that had been dormant for nearly four years: the rap star. Although he has moved in all sorts of directions since his start as a rapper, he still claims that music is closest to his heart. "The music career made everything else happen," he told the *Today* show. Will got back into the studio to record a couple of songs for the soundtrack, "Men in Black" and "Just Cruisin'." Will loved being behind the microphone after such a long absence, and judging from the sounds of those cool cuts, he hasn't lost his magic touch.

Upon the movie's opening, one hundred "Men in Black," dressed in the movie's trademark dark suit and Ray-Bans, stormed a Tower Records store in New York City to promote the CD. Mobs of fans waited while Will Smith signed copies of the soundtrack. In fact, that's not all Will signed. The man who thought his rapping days were over also inked an incredibly lucrative deal with Columbia Records.

On the single "Men in Black," Will raps over Patrice Rushen's 1980s hit "Forget Me Nots." The cut soared up both the pop and R&B charts.

The video put Will back in the spotlight on music-video channels, too. It features him mixing with the otherworldly much as he does in the movie: this time he dances with an alien creature. "The alien could dance," Will jokes but adds seriously that "this *Men in Black* thing has really . . . just opened my life up. It's opened my life and I'm letting that inner child run free."

Speaking of children, Will says that his real-life child is *MiB* crazy. He even jokes that after two megamovies featuring life in outer space, he's a little concerned about Trey's perception of reality. "I'm going to have to explain it to him. . . . Now, aliens are just for the movies, son. You know that, right?"

But does the world's biggest alien-buster *really* think that aliens can only be found in the movies? "I believe that it would be arrogant of us as humans to assume that we are the only beings that exist in this vast universe," he told Matt Lauer on the *Today* show, quickly adding, "I don't know if they have ships and attitude problems, but there's something out there."

Something may be "out there" as Smith says, but it's hard to imagine it being bigger than his career right now. While *ID4* catapulted Will into the realm of superstardom, *Men in Black* is proof that he's there to stay. He's definitely a man in demand: the magazine covers and talk shows featuring him have been endless. He's getting so many offers from so many studios that the buzz in Hollywood is that he may be its next $20 million man.

That incredible salary would put Will in the elite company of the richest movie stars ever: Harrison Ford, Mel Gibson, Jim Carrey, Arnold Schwarzenegger, and Sylvester Stallone.

His rap career is back on track, too, as singles from his first album in four years, *Big Willie Style*, climb up the billboard charts and a brand-new Grammy adorns his trophy case. No question, Will Smith's success is stellar. Like NBC Entertainment president Warren Littlefield has said: "Will Smith is a rocketship. He took off and just kept going."

15

BACK ATTACKIN' THE MIC

Big *Willie Style* in the fall of 1997 marked Will's full-on return to the music world. It was his first album in four years and the only one released under his real name. Although he parted with the Fresh Prince moniker this time out, he held on to his musical partner of many years, "Jazzy" Jeff Townes. Jeff produced three cuts on the album, including "It's All Good," "I Loved You," and "Don't Say Nothin'." He also also added his wax scratches to "Gettin' Jiggy Wit' It" and "Yes, Y'All." The duo even recorded the tracks in Jeff's home while taking breaks to play video games together, just as they did in the old days.

During Will's long hiatus from music, Smith's fans weren't the only ones anticipating his return. Will himself had been thinking about it for years. But the disappointing sales of *Code Red*, the feeling that he had said or rapped all that he had to say at the time, and the demands of his television and film career kept him away.

As time went on, however, he could hear the hip-hop world calling him back. Rapping was his first love. He had done it for most of his life, and it was, after all, the springboard for all his other successes in entertainment. It was a part of his life that simply would not go away.

After the deaths of Tupac Shakur and Biggie Smalls—two rappers Will very much admired—in 1997, Will was finally inspired to return to the field. The rap world had lost two very special talents and Will was determined not only to help fill the void, but also to give something back to the community that had given him so much at the start of his career. He had also done a lot of living in the four years that he had been away and felt once again that he had a lot to say. Fatherhood, divorce, new love, and fame were all life-altering forces that would influence his new music.

The opportunity to rap again came with the release of the *Men in Black* soundtrack—it was Will who performed the title song. It was as if getting behind the mic again jump-started him. It was all he needed to slip right back into the groove of writing and rapping. He immediately went to work on *Big Willie Style*, and the result was a smashing success.

The infectious "Gettin' Jiggy Wit' It" was the first single and video released from the album. In it, Will trades dancing with aliens for boogying with humans. And he proves to be a good dancer, too. In the "Jiggy" video, fans saw Will groove to Sister Sledge's hit of the late seventies, "He's the Greatest Dancer." Not only does the man get loose, he also wears some pretty stylin' suits and sportswear. Check out the Egyptian pharaoh garb!

Sister Sledge isn't the only group from the disco era Will gives props to. On "Candy," Will is backed by Cameo, the folks who originated the song "Good Times" by Chic, which is best known as the track that launched a million rap careers (you may recall that it was the backing track on the Sugar Hill Gang's seminal hit "Rapper Delight"), can be heard in "It's All Good." "Celebration" by Kool and the Gang is invoked in the same song. And the seventies supergroup Earth, Wind and Fire's "Something Special" resonates on the title track, "Big Willie Style."

Will pays homage to pre–disco era artists, too. He uses Stevie Wonder's "Ribbon in the Sky" on the harmonious "Chasing Forever," the Isley Brothers' "Here We Go Again" in "Yes, Y'All," and the Whispers' "And the Beat Goes On" in "Miami."

Why all the old stuff in *Big Willie Style*? Will has said that he hopes to spur a movement back to the good old days of rap and hip-hop with this album—the days of dancin', rhymin', and partyin', the days before the medium was tainted by incidents of violence. Of course, the best way for Smith to usher a return to rap's roots was to incorporate into his own work the songs that first influenced the genre. Will recently explained in *Entertainment Weekly* that in his view, "rap got away from its essence. The essence of rap was always about partying and having fun. The best rapper was the one that could rock the crowd. How well you shot a gun wasn't a part of the criteria." Will is eager to bring back that time, and *Big Willie Style* seems just the way to do it.

Will has also said that rap is still young. It has not yet completed its first growth cycle as rock and roll or jazz have. Hip-hop exploded in the eighties and nineties with a continuing stream of rap artists entering the arena. Taking this into account, he is optimistic that rap will come full circle as the millennium approaches and that the good-times sound represented in "Rapper's Delight" will indeed make a comeback. He predicts that other rappers will soon follow his lead and that hip-hop will actually start getting back to basics as soon as the summer of 1998.

After a four-year absence from the music world, anyone would have felt a little rusty behind the mic, but not Will Smith. Rhymes still rolled off his tongue like buttah, as the saying goes. What Will did feel, however, was a certain kind of pressure he had never felt before. The pressure isn't caused by his lucrative multialbum deal with Columbia Records, as one might suspect, he explains. The pressure actually comes from wanting to meet his own expectations. "It's more of an internal pressure. . . ." he told America Online. "I'm in a position financially where I don't have to say, 'Oh, I've got to sell five million albums.'. . . But my ego, which is the ultimate driving force . . . makes me want to sell twenty million records worldwide . . . so I'm driven by the ultimate drive now."

Only time will tell if *Big Willie Style* will indeed sell 20 million copies worldwide, but in the interim, the album has already cracked the top ten on both the R&B and pop charts, and has received critical acclaim, too. *Rolling Stone* said, "*Big Willie Style* is wickedly well conceived . . . the album crackles with the lucid energy of early 80s rap hits." The magazine also went on to tout the recording as "an exceptional mega-celebrity album." *USA Today* said, "Even when he's taking licks at his hip-hop detractors for his fun-loving style, his aim is to have a good time." *People* marveled that Smith "has somehow managed to stay in touch with his Philadelphia hip-hop roots. . . . The secret is a smooth syncopated vocal style that effortlessly nudges each song into soulful R&B territory without sacrificing danceability."

By any measure, Will Smith's big comeback album is a triumph that draws from everything he innately knows and has learned how to do well over the years. It is a collection of songs that is every bit as accessible and appealing as the megastar's performances on film and television have proven to be. Thanks to Columbia Records' backing, listeners who waited all this time to hear from Will again can now look forward to many more years of his music.

Owning the hot album *Big Willie Style* is a must for Will fans, not just because it features his funky dance tunes or because it takes us back to a cool time in the genre's history, but because it also contains lots of autobiographical material. As *Rolling Stone* points out, "Will Smith tells the story of his recent life with top flight perspective." Listeners will no doubt get a special feel for the man behind the music each and every time they listen to it.

Will not only dug deep for his inspiration, he dug wide—the tracks are as varied as Smith's movie roles have been. Four-part harmonies back Will up on "Chasing Forever," a love rap for his wife, Jada, while the lyrics of "I Loved You" conjure up images of a once brokenhearted superstar. Will also covers the subject of stardom in several cuts, including "Y'All Know," where he actually lists some of his accomplishments, "Yes, Y'All," where he explains the void he felt when he bowed out of rap for a while, and "Don't Say Nothin'," his answer to probing tabloids. Will also philosophizes in "It's All Good" that living and loving are the real keys to leading a happy life.

Listeners can't help bouncing along to "Miami," a rap with the catchy, bilingual refrain, "Welcome to Miami/Bienvenido a Miami." But Big Willie's favorite song is actually the touching "Just the Two of Us" because it's the most emotionally charged. The song deals with the subject of fatherhood and features Will rapping to his son, Trey, over Bill Withers's famous ballad. Will pleads to God, "Please let me be a good daddy," and pledges his life to Trey, whose voice can be heard on the track as well.

Despite the serious moments of personal insight, the album also features the megahit "Men in Black" (since, as Will likes to boast, it is the most played song in the history of rap) and also includes examples of Will's trademark sense of humor. Comedian Jamie Foxx appears on the album playing the part of an annoying reporter named Keith B-Real between cuts. Through Mr. Foxx's interludes, Will satirizes his critics. Foxx asks Will if he feels that he makes "real rap" music—a poke at those who said DJ Jazzy Jeff and the Fresh Prince made "bubblegum" rap. Foxx also pesters Will about his ego and grills him about his relationship with Jazzy Jeff—dashing gossip that the duo are no longer good friends.

Foxx isn't the only guest star on the album. In the liner notes, Will quotes the African proverb "It takes a village" as a thank-you to the many others who contributed to the album. In this case the other village members were rappers Left Eye and Camp Lo, pal "Jazzy" Jeff Townes, son, Trey, and wife, Jada.

So what's with the name, "Big Willie Style"? It's actually intended as a double entendre in the classic Will Smith style. In addition to being a playful variation on Smith's first name, a "Willie" in street slang is someone who lives large, who has a lot of flashy cars, and big money to spend. Will explained to *USA Today* that "in the hip slang, a Willie is somebody who is the man. I thought about what rappers are talking about—having nice cars, private jets, fancy houses and all that—and how that makes them a Willie. So I termed myself the big Williest because the life a lot of those people are fantasizing about is the life I'm living."

There's no question that Will Smith is the ultimate "Big Willie," but in assuming the title, Smith adds a twist to its definition. "Being a Big Willie is based on other things. So-called Willies used different measuring tools than I use," he explains. "For me the ultimate Willie tool, the Willie measuring stick, the Willie litmus test, is intellect."

In true Big Willie style, Smith ends the thank-you section of his album notes with a very telling comment. It reads, "And I want you all to know that I'm very clear that no one becomes 'The Big Williest' by themselves."

Will often credits God, his family, and his friends with helping him become the person he is today. But he makes his true inspiration clear to the world when he writes, ". . . to Trey and Jada, I live, love and work, every second of the day hoping to make you proud of who I am. I love you."

Once again Will Smith proves that he's got what it takes to make it in the music world. His determination, skill, and love of what he does are what make him a success across so many fields of entertainment. To fans who ask Will how to make it in the hip-hop biz, he has this advice: "You gotta love hip-hop and not money. You've gotta do it 'cause it's something that you love from the heart and not something about getting paid. And if you keep doing it—and if you keep loving it—then you can't help but be successful."

16

THE SECRETS OF HIS SUCCESS

Few careers have taken off like Will Smith's. Even fewer talents have had success in three different fields! Will has excelled in music, television, *and* film. It's hard to imagine how any human could accomplish so much at such a young age.

Professionally, Will's achievements are astounding. He's won three Grammys and two American Music Awards for his rap records. He was nominated for a Golden Globe for his performance on *The Fresh Prince of Bel-Air*. He's garnered two NAACP Image awards, one as a rap artist, and one for Best Comedy Series. He was also named a ShoWest Male Star of Tomorrow, and Best Male Newcomer for *Bad Boys* by Blockbuster Entertainment in 1996.

And the honors don't stop there: In 1997 alone he received a Hall of Fame award from the Nickelodeon Kids' Choice awards; a Blockbuster award for Best Male Actor in a Science Fiction Role for *ID4*; the ShoWest award for International Box Office Achievement; an MTV Movie Award nomination for Best Male Performance for *ID4*, and MTV awards for "best kiss" with Vivica Fox in *ID4* and for Best Song from a Movie for *Men in Black* and an MTV Music Video award for Best Video for a Film, *Men in Black*. The list keeps growing, too. VH1 gave him a fashion award for Best Personal Style, Male, and he's been nominated for another American Music Award, two more NAACP Awards, and two more Blockbuster Entertainment Awards. Also the People's Choice Awards nominated Will for Best Actor against heavyweights Harrison Ford and Tom Cruise.

What could possibly be next for Will Smith's already crowded trophy shelf? Is there room for an Oscar?

And just what *is* the secret of Smith's success? Is there a magic formula? It's clear that he is a hard worker, who is committed, focused, and dedicated to whatever he pursues. "I can't stand not having anything to do when I get up in the morning," he says.

Smith also believes deeply in himself and his abilities. "I am extremely confident in who I am," he says, and adds that "confidence is what makes me different from guys at home."

It's this well of self-assurance that allows

him to take risks. Philadelphia 76er Julius "Dr. J" Erving inspired Will to cross his fingers and go for it. "Dr. J says, 'When the ball is [yours] in the fourth quarter, always take the shot.' I always take the shot," Will says.

Will has often used basketball metaphors to explain his success. Even back in 1990, he told *Vanity Fair:* "I know personally fifteen people who could do exactly what I'm doing right now. But they're scared to take that shot. If they give me the position, I'll shoot my shot. The only thing that can go wrong is, I miss. And if I miss, I'll shoot again."

Add drive and unbridled energy to self-confidence and risk taking, and the Smith formula for success is complete. "It's a plus to me that people are lazy," he said in the *New York Times.* "I take comfort in knowing that even if someone's more talented, a better rapper or actor than I am, they're not going to put in the hours I put in. I have this really psychotic drive," he admits. "I can't sleep, I can't eat, until what I start is finished to the best of my ability."

How does Will account for his mass appeal? He is convinced people love him because he likes "to have fun. I like to be silly, make jokes, and people enjoy that. . . . So, when the camera's turned on and I'm having fun, people can see that, people can feel that when they watch the movie."

Will's sense of fun carries through no

matter what kind of film he happens to be making. "It should always have a sense of humor. No matter how painful the situation you're dealing with, there should be humor to it because that gives people hope."

Will says this is why audiences "let me in. In general, the things I like tend to fit perfectly with the mainstream." He's right. His audiences include males and females of all ages and races.

Industry insiders have their own theories as to why Will is red hot. Roland Emmerich, the director of *Independence Day*, speculates that audiences love Will Smith because "there is something very masculine about Will that makes him believable as a hero."

Director Barry Sonnenfeld of *MiB* says movie-watchers succumb to Will-power because Smith is "incredibly self-confident and normal." Sonnenfeld has been known to say that he never wants to make a movie again without Will.

Dean Devlin, the producer for *Independence Day*, thinks that audiences can't get enough of Smith because he is a lot like his Captain Hiller character. "He's really an all-American guy; he stands for all that's good. He's like that in real life, too. He had success at an early age and yet he didn't become an egomaniac; he's the sweetest, most real guy you could meet."

But Will disagrees, saying that he actually

does have a big ego. "You have to have a big ego to be an actor," he explained to *Vibe Online*. "But I have control over that because I don't like how it feels when other people throw their weight around. That experience makes me struggle really hard not to impose myself on people for selfish reasons. Ego drives you. I think it's really important. But you have to control your ego; you can't let your ego control you."

How does Hollywood's hottest star prevent this "big ego" from exploding? "I've already been a success," he notes. "It has already gone to my head. I've already been selfish—didn't listen to anyone."

Being famous at a young age allowed Smith to be foolish and to make some mistakes, but he had the intelligence and drive to overcome them. "I had a period in my life where I sought the attention, had a little money . . . and all that type of stuff. But the real person inside me just dictated how I had to act, how I had to behave and how I had to treat people," he told *Newsday*.

Will also credits his parents' values and examples with helping him keep his feet on the ground. "My parents and my upbringing outweighed the temptations of Hollywood, the glitter, the money, and all that." He adds firmly, "Who I really am wins every time."

Coming from the sometimes undependable music industry taught Smith how to rely on himself. Though he recognizes that Hollywood is tough, he thinks the music biz is even more cutthroat. "When I had a hit album, everything at the record company was great and wonderful. When one flopped, they wouldn't even take my phone calls. From that you learn to depend on yourself. You learn not to allow your successes to go to your head and not to allow your failures to go to your heart. I was prepared for all that by the time I made it into television and, now, into films."

Choosing the right roles is also an important part of the process. "I look for trends." Smith knew *Independence Day* would be a hit because he "looked at the top ten movies of all time, and seven of the top ten had creatures in them. You had *E.T.*, *Jurassic Park*, *Close Encounters*, *Jaws*," he reasoned.

Smith says he wants to continue to play positive characters. "I want to play characters that represent really strong, positive black images. So that's the thing I consider when I'm taking a role after I decide if it's something that I want to do."

Since fame and fortune came to him so quickly, Smith says he's not afraid of failure. He keeps it in perspective. "There's going to be a time when it's over. . . . And being sure who you are helps you get through that. There will always be something I can do."

When asked about his philosophy of his success, Will half-jokes, "You know, I don't even think about how I got here anymore. It just sort of happened."

But when pressed, he confides that he truly feels blessed. "I'm very comfortable with my life, and I'm very comfortable with life in general. I think that if you put out good energy, you get good energy back. I just try to constantly put out good energy, and it comes back tenfold."

17

BEHIND THE SHADES: THE REAL WILL SMITH

He's a cool, confident cutup with a quick quip onscreen. But what's the private Will Smith like once the Ray-Bans are off and the big guns are down? Would you be surprised to discover that Smith actually shares a lot of the same characteristics as his onscreen creations?

Obviously, he has the most in common with the Fresh Prince. Though he has grown up tremendously since those days, he still has a lot of the bouncy rapper in him, and enjoys jamming to the sounds of the Fugees, Biggie Smalls, LL Cool J, and Tupac.

Smith shares a home, an hour north of Los Angeles, with his wife, actress Jada Pinkett, and four dogs. The property includes a stream, a swimming pool, a recording studio, and a golf hole so he can practice his favorite pastime.

His home was described as "impressive, yet not ostentatious" by *Newsweek*. The article points out "soft fabrics around the windows . . . African masks and pretty decorative objects." Family photos hang from the walls and are strewn about on tabletops.

The "sprawling" home is called "La Hacienda," *Essence* magazine reports, describing it as a "ranch-style property" with courtyards, an atrium, and "rich cobblestone floors." *Essence* also says that the house exudes an "airy, peaceful feeling."

Smith's four 140-pound rottweilers frolic around the property. Two were a gift from *Tonight* show host Jay Leno. Smith adored the pups so much that he bought two more.

Smith, ever the proud dad, spends as much time with his son, Trey, as he can. The two like to play games together, and Will hopes to interest his son in some of his hobbies, which include playing chess as well as golf.

Will's own father taught him how to play chess when he was eight years old, and he thought their games were terrific father–son bonding experiences. Will says that both chess and golf "teach you self-control and patience. If you allow your passion to take you over and have its way with you, you can't win."

Although Smith enjoys a wide variety of sports, including bowling, pool, basketball, and racquetball, golf is number one. He calls it the "ultimate sport" and the "best metaphor for life that there is in sports. Through those eighteen holes, you're up, you're down. You hit a bad shot, you're out. But your next shot is incredible, and you're back in it again. You can play golf with someone and tell what kind of person they are without ever hearing them talk."

Smith has been seen on the links with Tiger Woods and Michael Jordan. He likes to joke that Tiger is one of the "aliens" among us on Earth, because of his extraordinary ability on the green. But Will considers playing against himself "the most fierce competition on the planet."

18

THE FRESH PRINCE AND HIS PRINCESS

Will appeared to have everything one might need to be happy—success, popularity, a great family, and a job he loved. But he was still an old-fashioned guy and lived by the adage that every king *does* need a queen. He finally found his queen of hearts in the beautiful young actress Jada Pinkett, and after a long courtship, Will married the woman of his dreams. He's not the only one smitten by Jada, either. With her red-hot acting career, she's heating up the screen at an alarming rate.

Will Smith and Jada Pinkett tied the knot on December 31, 1997, in an ultraprivate New Year's Eve ceremony held at the Cloisters, a breathtaking mansion just outside of Jada's hometown of Baltimore, Maryland. The nuptials were so hush-hush that the 125 guests were whisked to the ceremony in limousines without knowing their destination.

Mr. and Mrs. Smith successfully kept the media at bay for a while, but the tabloids were still able to glean enough details about the superstar wedding to make it front-page news. Will was reportedly very generous, spending in excess of $3 million on the fete, not including the $250,000 diamond wedding ring for Jada, and the brand-new Ferrari it is said that he gave her as a wedding present. It is Jada's first marriage, and she was apparently quite the blushing—and sexy—bride, wearing a stunning high-neck, off-white lace gown by designer Badgley Mischka.

The bride and groom exchanged their vows in the form of love letters by the light of three hundred candles. Love was in the air, as was the scent of exotic flowers flown in from all around the world. Will's young son, Trey, his young nephew, and Jada's young goddaughter preceded the couple down the aisle as their wedding party. Among the many family and friends in attendance at the elegant wedding were Jasmine Guy (*A Different World*) and Tisha Campbell (*Martin*).

Just what kind of music do a rap star and his lovely bride play at their wedding? A touch of everything is the answer. A disc jockey provided most of the evening's music, but the a cappella group Infinity also performed. (Yes, Will sang, too. The tune was "Gettin' Jiggy Wit' It.")

The couple then spent the night in a luxury hotel overlooking Baltimore's Inner Harbor. After the New Year, they were spotted honeymooning—and still celebrating—in Miami, one of Will's favorite cities. The blissful lovebirds were seen dancing the night away in chic South Beach hot spots, including the very hip club Chaos. It seems they have a lot to be happy about. The couple are expecting a child in July 1998.

Hollywood began media speculating about a Pinkett–Smith wedding when they first started dating in 1995. And though the tabloids were asking, "*Will* he or won't he?" for quite some time, the loving couple moved at their own pace. They refused to let the press rush them. Jada claims that even her pregnancy didn't speed things up. In fact, she told *People* magazine, ". . . one day we got engaged, and the next we found out we were pregnant."

So who exactly is this lucky woman? The one Tinseltown's fastest-rising star fell in love with and married? Obviously, Jada Pinkett is a very special lady.

Jada was bitten by the performing bug at an early age. She attended the prestigious Baltimore School for the Arts, where she studied dance and choreography, and then continued at the North Carolina School for the Arts, where she majored in theater.

In 1991 Jada landed her first big acting job on the television sitcom *A Different World*.

From there she made the leap to the big screen, much as Will did. Her career has also taken off at a gallop.

The first movie she made was *Menace II Society* (1993). Her magnetic appeal led her to land three more films in 1994: *A Low Down Dirty Shame*, *Jason's Lyric*, and *The Inkwell*. But it wasn't until 1996 that Hollywood knew it had a real superstar on its hands. Audiences loved her as Eddie Murphy's romantic interest in the hit remake of *The Nutty Professor*, and as Stony in the fem-powered *Set It Off*. Jada's star rose even higher when she appeared in *Scream 2*, winning her rave reviews for her performance.

From that point on, producers scrambled to sign up the pint-size beauty for starring roles. She's slated to play two leading parts in 1998. First up is *Woo*, in which Jada stars with Isaac Hayes, LL Cool J, and comeback queen Pam Grier. *Force Majeure*, an action-thriller, co-starring Anne Heche, Joaquin Phoenix, and Vince Vaughan, follows quickly on *Woo*'s heels. Under the direction of Joseph Ruben (*Money Train*), *Force Majeure* promises to deliver.

In addition to acting, Jada has many other talents. She continues to dance and write poetry. She is even one up on her hubby—she has worked behind the camera, too. Jada has directed music videos for Gerald Levert, Maxine Harvey, and MC Lyte. And it doesn't end there. Jada also has a clothing line for petite women called Maja!

It's no wonder that Will feels he met his match in this multitalented superwoman. The two laid eyes on each other for the first time when Jada auditioned for the role of Will's girlfriend on *The Fresh Prince of Bel Air.* She didn't get the part because the casting director thought she was too short. In real life, Will doesn't mind towering more than a foot over his petite princess.

Though Jada didn't work with Will on *Fresh Prince*, they got to know each other through mutual friends, and eventually they became friends themselves. It was when Will was going through his divorce, however, that the two grew so close. Jada was there to console Will and soon the friendship blossomed into romance. As Jada now says, "There's nothing I can't say to him, nothing I can't share."

It was that emotional connection that made Will fall hard for Jada. "She's very in touch with her emotions, which allows me to be in touch with mine. She helps me deal with everything I have to deal with. She makes everything okay. No matter how difficult it gets, she always has something kind to say or a warm hug," he told *Ebony* magazine.

Will also says that he is attracted to Jada's brains, calling her "an intellectual goddess." A romantic at heart, Will likes to spoil Jada with massages, sponge baths, red wine, and candle-light picnics. One of Will's favorite gifts to Jada was awakening her on her birthday with a Mexican mariachi band serenading her with "Amore."

Will adds that Jada is his best friend and "soul mate," and he feels that their relationship works particularly well because she understands the demands of being an actor. "Actors hook up out of necessity. The beauty of my life with Jada is that what happened with my first marriage wouldn't make Jada panic. She understands that place. It takes a really special understanding. Jada, being an actress, and just being so completely brilliant, she understands fame, she understands fans, having money, not having money, a success-ful creative endeavor versus an unsuccessful creative endeavor and how that affects you psychologically and emotionally. She under-stands what I do."

It's clear that Jada's feelings for Will are intense as well. She says that her man is thoughtful and she had "never had some-one who was so familiar. Our lives are so parallel and our ideas and our philosophies—everything just matches." She adores Will's sense of humor, saying, "I cannot imagine being on this planet with anybody else."

The couple are so close that they've written a screenplay together, called *Love for Hire*. Universal Pictures bought the script in the blink of an eye. Soon the romantic duo will have a chance to make their chemistry work onscreen as well as off. They will costar in the flick, which is set to start filming in 1998.

The Fresh Prince has found his Princess in Jada Pinkett, and complete happiness in his new married life. Will says his lady love has put it all in perspective, teaching him that "life is really the most important thing . . . a big movie and all of that is fun—you can enjoy that, and Hollywood premieres—but your life and your family are what's really important."

19

WILL SMITH, THE NEXT PRESIDENT OF THE UNITED STATES

In 1998 Will Smith will be the busiest man in Hollywood. Countless offers have poured in, and he has already committed himself to movie, music, and producing endeavors.

Like many successful actors, Will has his own production company, Will Smith Enterprises, through which he will further explore film, music, and television. He is currently working on recording projects with singers Tatyana Ali, costar of *The Fresh Prince of Bel-Air*, and Tichina Arnold.

In fact, Will Smith Enterprises is currently negotiating with Universal to create a multimedia company where Will would be the driving force behind movies, music, and television shows.

Will is also thrilled to be recording music himself again. The *Men in Black* soundtrack and *Big Willie Style* highlighted his skill for bustin' rhymes, and the lucrative multialbum deal with Columbia Records guarantees that he will be kicking out more jams in the near future.

But Big Willie's biggest plans right now are film-related. In 1998, fans may be able to see him in as many as four movies. No doubt the studios will try to strike while Will is red-hot.

First up is *Enemy of the State*, in which Will costars with Gene Hackman. In this political conspiracy thriller, Will portrays a wrongfully persecuted target of a national security agent. He spent the fall of 1997 and early 1998 filming *Enemy* in Los Angeles, Washington, and Baltimore. Along with Hackman, costars include esteemed film vets Jason Robards and Jon Voight.

Enemy of the State promises to be a departure for Will, who feels that variety is the key to big-screen success. It's his first thriller, and the word on the street is that the role requires Smith to leave his sense of humor at the door. No doubt he will draw on the dramatic talent he used in *Six Degrees of Separation*.

Jerry Bruckheimer (*Bad Boys*) is signed on as the producer, and Tony Scott, known for *Beverly Hills Cop II* and the Tom Cruise smashes *Days of Thunder* and *Top Gun*, will direct. With a team like this, *Enemy of the State* is positioned to be the hot summer movie of 1998. A whole lot of people are hoping that this will be the third blockbuster in a row for Smith.

Next up for Will is Barry Sonnenfeld's *Wild, Wild West*, for which Will will receive a cool $15 million. His costar is rumored to be Kevin Kline, replacing heartthrob George Clooney, who dropped out. If the title sounds familiar, that's because it is: *Wild, Wild West* was a popular CBS television series that ran from 1965 to 1970. Focusing on the lives of federal agents in the cowboy days of the 1870s, the series was part Western, part spy adventure, and part science fiction.

Smith is slated to play ladies' man James T. West, the role originated by Robert Conrad on TV. There are reports that Conrad is thinking about appearing in the film too, but this time as President Ulysses S. Grant. Kevin Kline would play Artemus Gordon, master of disguise.

Fans of gadgetry, humor, and action are sure to get their fill in *Wild, Wild West*. In fact, the TV series was so full of action, particularly shoot-outs and barroom brawls, that Frank Stanton, then president of CBS, pulled it off the air as part of his pledge to Congress to reduce television violence. By today's standards, those fight scenes were tame. Just for fun, *Wild, Wild West* fans should catch the reruns in syndication on TNT before or after they see the movie.

Wild, Wild West, the movie, started shooting in April 1998 and was originally slated for a summer 1999 release, but the plan now is to move that date up to the end of 1998 because of all the positive buzz the production has been getting.

Will calls *Love for Hire*, the project after *Wild, Wild West*, "a romantic comedy about a busy woman lawyer who decides she wants a baby but doesn't want the hassle of a man." Will will play the construction worker/hired "stud" who has a change of heart about the agreement later. "It was our first time working together," Will told *USA Today*, then adds, "I think I had more fun than she [Jada] did. I'm a psychotic workaholic, doing 12- to 14-hour days. We were sitting in a room and realized that three days had passed and we hadn't seen the sun."

Brian Grazer, producer of such recent hits as Jim Carrey's *Liar, Liar* and Mel Gibson's *Ransom*, is set to produce. Grazer, who worked with Jada on *The Nutty Professor*, jumped at the chance to work with her again. Imagine Entertainment reports a 1999 release.

And for those of you who just love movies where Will saves the world, he's about to do it for a third time! Smith reportedly just signed on for a film called *The Mark*, which, like *Men in Black*, is based on a popular comic book. In it, Smith will play a reluctant hero who inadvertently gains powers from an ancient talisman, then must struggle to save the world from doom. That's our Will.

And don't forget the sequels: *Bad Boys 2* is expected in early 1999, with filming set in Miami and London. Martin Lawrence will also return. Will has publicly said that he's "very interested" in sequels to *Independence Day* and *Men in Black.* "If they come up with a good script, I'm there," he said.

There's also talk of Will starring in two biopics down the line. One is about jazz composer Billy Strayhorn, based on the book *Lush Life.* The other is the story of boxing great Muhammad Ali. When Smith met the former champ, he said, Ali "looked me up and down and said: 'You're almost as pretty as me, so it might work.'"

Other possibilities for the Man-in-Millions include *Brushback*, a time-travel film about a major-league baseball player who goes back to play in the Negro Leagues. Will's good friend Benny Medina, the creator of *The Fresh Prince of Bel-Air*, is said to be attached to the project, with John Singleton directing.

When asked who he'd like to work with in the future, Will mentions director Martin Scorcese, and actress Jennifer Lopez, whose performance in *Selena* wowed him.

What else could be next for this man of many talents? "I want to be the first black president," Will Smith declares. "Give me about ten years, I'm going to run for president. If I can squeeze in an NBA championship before that, I'll do it."

20

HIS FUTURE'S SO BRIGHT . . .

There's no question that Will Smith is the hottest sensation the entertainment industry has seen in years. He soared onto the music charts just ten years ago, as half of a dynamic rap duo. He brought his brand of hip-hop humor to America's living rooms every week on the top-rated comedy series *The Fresh Prince of Bel-Air*. Then he burst onto the big screen with his breakout performance in *Six Degrees of Separation*; he kicked butt, human and alien, in *Bad Boys* and *Independence Day*; and made "Please look directly into the neuralyzer" a household phrase in *Men in Black*.

His box-office power proves that he has joined the ranks of the world's biggest stars. Yet the man behind all this fame is remarkably humble, humorous, and happy. He has never forgotten the values and focus that his parents taught him; he will never forget his home, family, and people close to his heart.

Fatherhood turned him into a real man, and that's no doubt part of what attracted his lovebird, Jada Pinkett. Will's love of laughter and life is perhaps what has made him most attractive to the rest of the world.

Will Smith's star is shining bright. As bright as the sun his cool Ray-Bans protect him from. He doesn't have any plans for an early retirement, that's for sure. Fans who thrive on Will-power will be able to get it for years to come.

WILL SMITH: JUST THE FACTS

NAME: Willard C. Smith II
OCCUPATION: Rapper, actor
BIRTH DATE: September 25, 1968
BIRTHPLACE: Philadelphia, Pennsylvania
STAR SIGN: Sun in Libra, moon in Scorpio
HEIGHT: 6 feet, 2 inches
WEIGHT: 206 pounds
HOME: Ventura County, California
PARENTS: Carolyn and Willard Smith, Sr.
SIBLINGS: Pam, Ellen, and Harry
PETS: Four rottweilers
MARITAL STATUS: Divorced from Sheree Zampino; married to actress Jada Pinkett
CHILDREN: Son, Willard C. Smith III, nicknamed Trey, born December 1992; another child due in July 1998.
EDUCATION: High school
HOBBIES: Golfing; shooting pool; playing basketball, racquetball, chess
INFLUENCES: Julius "Dr. J" Erving; Eddie Murphy; parents
LITTLE-KNOWN CAMEO APPEARANCES: On the television series *Blossom*, in 1991; in the movie *A Thin Line Between Love and Hate* (1996)
FAVORITE RAPPERS: The Fugees, Biggie Smalls, LL Cool J, Tupac, Run DMC

WHAT'S ON WILL'S MIND

ON THE APPEAL OF ACTION HEROES:
"That whole super-guy thing, the super-macho man who jumps in front of a bullet just to be tough, is not appealing. It's more appealing when you duck."

ON RELATIONSHIPS:
"I don't start relationships with people quickly. I take a long time to get to know someone. I'm always honest; we can hang out, we can do things, but I need time."

ON JADA:
"Jada Pinkett is my best friend. Not my best *female* friend. She's my best friend, period. And that's the only way a relationship can work."

ON BEING A BLACK ROLE MODEL:
"There are so few successful black actors in comparison with Caucasian actors that every move you make is like a step for your people. That's a bit much. But I try not to focus on it. My only real litmus test is: Will my mother be embarrassed by the work I've done? As long as my family isn't embarrassed, it generally works out for my people, too."

ON THE WAR ON DRUGS:

"Fighting the drug battle in the streets is the wrong place. Our government could stop it if they wanted to. With all the technology we saw in the [Persian] gulf that helped win the war, I can't believe they can't stop drugs coming in from Colombia."

ON HIS SMOOTH-TALKING STYLE:

"I talk a good game. Jeff [Townes] would say that each time I talk, it just keeps getting bigger and bigger. When I get into an argument, I keep trying to convince the other person that I'm right. I can just keep talking and talking. The other person will never win. Even if the other person knows that he is right, I'll just keep talking and talking until the other person gives up."

ON WHAT HE LIKED MOST ABOUT THE FRESH PRINCE OF BEL-AIR:

"What I am happiest about is that I could be a role model and give people something to think about. It's important to have a black show that's positive."

ON WHY PEOPLE LIKE HIM:

"It's the ears! Americans have an ear fetish. Absolutely. Americans love people with big ears—Mickey Mouse, Goofy, Dumbo, Ross Perot. Americans love ears."

ON HIS PERSONALITY:

"I'm just outgoing. I'm comfortable enough to impose myself on my surroundings. That's the best way to describe it, really. It's a gift. It's the ability to impose myself on my surroundings without making people feel imposed upon."

ON RACISM IN HOLLYWOOD:

"I think there is racism in every aspect of American culture and life, so why would we think it would be any different [in Hollywood]? It's a part of living in our world and it's something that, unfortunately, we all have to deal with. I think it's a cancer that erodes the very base of our existence."

ON WHO MAKES HIM TONGUE-TIED:

"Quincy Jones does it to me the most. You don't feel like you should say anything if Quincy's talking. When he's finished, clap. Now, *he's* deep."

ON THE DIFFERENCE BETWEEN DOING TV AND MOVIES:

"[In] doing TV comedy, you work so hard to maximize every single individual second; when you get to do a movie, you have all the time you need. 'What? You mean I can try fifteen or twenty different options?' You gotta love that!"

ON GROWING UP:

"When I was younger, it was more about being different when everyone else wanted to fit in. I always wanted how I talked or my clothes to be different. Peer pressure never meant anything to me. If something was done one way, something in me resisted it."

ON WHAT HE WOULD HAVE DONE IF HE HADN'T BECOME A RAPPER:

"I probably would have gone to college. I had a scholarship to MIT. I probably would have studied computer engineering. I was always really good at math. I love to invent things, so I might have been the guy that invented the TV remote control, or something like that, if I had been around back then."

ON *INDEPENDENCE DAY*:

"This is a disaster film in the classic sense, with a great, massive cast. When the movie starts, you don't know who is going to be around at the end of the film. These types of films haven't been made much recently, but I grew up watching them, and it's fun to be in one."

AWARDS AND HONORS

1988: Grammy Award for Best Rap Performance ("Parents Just Don't Understand")

1988: American Music Award for Best New Artist ("Parents")

1989: MTV Music Video Award for Best Rap Video

1991: Grammy Award for Best Rap Performance by a Duo or Group ("Summertime")

1991: American Music Award for Best Rap Performance ("Summertime")

1992: Golden Globe nomination for Best Performance by an Actor in a Television Series

1992: NAACP Image Award for Outstanding Rap Artist

1992: NAACP Image Award for Best Comedy Series

1995: ShoWest Award for Male Star of Tomorrow

1996: Blockbuster Entertainment Award for Best Male Newcomer in Action/Comedy (*Bad Boys*)

1996: NAACP Image Award nomination for Outstanding Lead Actor in a Comedy Series

1996: NAACP Image Award nomination for Outstanding Comedy Series

1996: MTV Movie Award nomination for Best On-Screen Duo (*Bad Boys*)

1997: Blockbuster Entertainment Award for Best Male Actor in Science Fiction Role (*ID4*)

1997: Nickelodeon Kids' Choice Hall of Fame Award

1997: ShoWest Award for International Box Office Achievement

1997: MTV Movie Award for Best Kiss (with Vivica Fox, *ID4*)

1997: People's Choice Award for Favorite Dramatic Movie (*ID4*)

1997: MTV Movie Award for Best Song from a Movie (*MiB*)

1997: MTV Music Video Award for Best Video for a Film (*MiB*)

1997: VH1 Fashion Award for Best Personal Style, Male

1997: Golden Globe nomination, Best Picture, Comedy/Musical (*MiB*)

1997: Blockbuster Entertainment Award nomination for Favorite Soundtrack (*MiB*)

1997: NAACP Image Award nomination for Outstanding Rap Artist (*MiB*)

1997: NAACP Image Award nomination for Outstanding Music Video (*MiB*)

1997: American Music Award nomination for Favorite Soundtrack (*MiB*)

1997: People's Choice Award nomination for Best Actor (*MiB*)

1998: Grammy Award for Best Rap Solo Performance (*MiB*)

DISCOGRAPHY

ALBUMS:
DJ JAZZY JEFF AND THE FRESH PRINCE
Rock the House (1987)
He's the DJ, I'm the Rapper (1988)
And In This Corner (1989)
Homebase (1991)
Code Red (1993)

WILL SMITH
Big Willie Style (1997)

SINGLES:
DJ JAZZY JEFF AND THE FRESH PRINCE
"Girls Ain't Nothing But Trouble" (1986)
"The Magnificent Jazzy Jeff" (1987)
"A Touch of Jazz" (1987)
"Parents Just Don't Understand" (1988)
"I Think I Can Beat Mike Tyson" (1989)
"Summertime" (1991)
"Ring My Bell" (1993)
"Boom! Shake the Room" (1993)

WILL SMITH
"Men in Black" (1997)
"Just Cruisin'" (1997)
"Gettin' Jiggy Wit' It" (1997)

TELEVISION APPEARANCES

Disneyland's 35th Anniversary Celebration (1989)
The Fresh Prince of Bel-Air (1990–96)
Blossom (cameo) (1991)
MTV Spring Break cohost (1995)

FILMOGRAPHY

Where the Day Takes You (1992)
Made in America (1993)
Six Degrees of Separation (1993)
Bad Boys (1995)
Independence Day (1996)
A Thin Line Between Love and Hate (cameo) (1996)
Men in Black (1997)
Enemy of the State (1998)
Wild, Wild West (1998)
Bad Boys 2 (1999)
Love for Hire (1999)
The Mark (1999)
Anything for Love (tentatively 1999)

WHERE TO WRITE

Will Smith
330 Bob Hope Drive
Burbank, CA 91523

Will Smith
c/o CAA
9830 Wilshire Blvd.
Beverly Hills, CA 90212

Will Smith's Official Website:
http://www.willsmith.net

GRAND SLAM STARS: MARTINA HINGIS AND VENUS WILLIAMS
by Michael Teitelbaum

They played face to face in the youngest matchup ever in a Grand Slam final. Now Martina Hingis and Venus Williams are together again—in a back-to-back bio!

AND

THE BACKSTREET BOYS
by K. S. Rodriguez

They're famous, they're hot, and now they're totally yours! Pick up this bio and let the story of the Backstreet Boys drive you wild!

Both from

HA!
Harper
Active™

A Division of HarperCollinsPublishers